Growing Up in

GULFPORT

Growing Up in
GULFPORT

*Boomer Memories from Stone's Ice Cream
to Johnny Elmer and the Rockets*

JOHN CUEVAS

THE
History
PRESS

Published by The History Press
Charleston, SC
www.historypress.com

All images are from the author's collection unless otherwise noted.

First published 2019

Manufactured in the United States

ISBN 9781467144087

Library of Congress Control Number: 2019945295

CONTENTS

INTRODUCTION

I recently moved back to my old hometown of Gulfport, Mississippi, after having lived in Atlanta for over fifty years. I arrived in the evening, driving past the bright lights and dazzling hotels of the Gulf Coast's new casino row. My thoughts went back to the nightspots we knew on the Biloxi strip. It wasn't Las Vegas by any means, and we didn't have the large, glitzy casinos that stretch along the coast today, but to a teenager who enjoyed cruising Beach Boulevard in the 1950s, the atmosphere was just as exciting.

Growing up in Gulfport was not like living in any other part of the state. The coast not only had commerce, it also had nightlife. The nightclubs, bars, strip clubs, illegal booze and open gambling kept the coast towns rocking long after other small towns were fast asleep.

On my first night back in Gulfport, I opened the windows of my room to hear the chirping of crickets, a sound I had almost forgotten after so many years in the big city. This tiny chorus welcomed me home and reminded me of the simple fun we used to have…spinning around in the backyard with our friends until we fell down dizzy with delight, giggling so much we could hardly catch our breath; lying on our backs imagining the most wonderful shapes in the puffy white clouds as they drifted past us in the blue summer sky; chasing after the small lightning bugs that sparkled like floating diamonds in the night, blinking on and off, playing hide-and-seek with us while we tried to capture them in a jar; and playing outside until the streetlights came on or our mothers called us home for supper.

As I listened to the syncopated chirps of the cricket chorus, I could feel the humid air, thick like the oozing glob of a lava lamp slowly rising in the heat. The steamy dampness reminded me of the long summer nights in Gulfport as a child lying in bed, twisting and turning, trying every way to fall asleep, aware of the clammy feeling of the sheets, while trying to survive the moist, oppressive heat. I would eventually be lulled to sleep by the whirring sound of an Emerson fan oscillating to and fro on the nightstand nearby and the choir of tiny frogs outside praying for rain—the stifling humidity of the Mississippi Gulf Coast that now, even with air conditioning, seems at times impossible to tolerate. Back then, our most efficient methods of cooling down on a hot summer day were running through the spray of a backyard garden hose or spending an afternoon at the Hotel Markham swimming pool.

When I awoke on that first morning back, the ground was damp from a cool overnight rain and the sun was struggling to peek through a heavy layer of fog that had rolled in from the Gulf. I almost expected to see Vampira, the horror movie hostess, appear out of the gray mist with her black hair and pencil-thin waist or to hear Morgus the Magnificent calling for Chopsley in a vignette from the "House of Shock."

Foggy morning on the coast.

Mosquito trucks spewed out clouds of endless joy.

The thick fog reminded me of those evenings at twilight, when the neighborhood kids would run behind the glorious mosquito trucks, those slow-moving contraptions rattling along, spewing out clouds of endless joy as we darted in and out of the thick gray smoke. The compelling smell of Malathion spewing forth from the machines tinged the evening air, drawing us to the trucks like moths to a flame. No one at the time seemed to question the potential hazard to our health.

Many of us who grew up in Gulfport have warm memories not only of the way downtown used to be, with its thriving businesses and bustling streets, but also of sunsets over the water, high school bonfires on the beach, sock hops in the gym, floundering in the Gulf, submarine races at the rock pile, fiesta at the Fiesta, dark corners in the Julep Room, Johnny Elmer and the Rockets at the yacht club, rum and coke at the White Cap, Wheel Burgers at Spiders, a cold beer at Elsie's, a spearmint snowball at the Pop Corn King, calling home for a ride from Jones Brothers Drug Store, riding the only escalator on the coast at the new Sears store and walking through the flock of pigeons strutting among the shoppers as if they were about to board one of the buses lined up in front of McCrory's. For some of us who grew up during those times, it was far more than just a simpler way of life; in retrospect, Gulfport was special.

We grew up in Gulfport during a time when medicines came without safety caps because it would have never crossed our minds to poison a perfect stranger. A time when we never had to look for our keys; they were always in the car, more often than not in the ignition. A time when our front

Jones Brothers Drugstore.

doors were hardly ever locked. A time when Little League had tryouts and not everyone made the team. A time when a gas station was a real service station, a place where you would get your oil checked, your gas pumped, your tires inflated and your windshield cleaned all without asking; the air for the tires was free, and many stations even gave S&H green stamps as a bonus. A time when the ultimate dream car was a 1957 Chevy to cruise up and down the beach from the Point in Biloxi to the tollbooth at the Bay St. Louis bridge and back again, to peel out, lay rubber or go to the rock pile in Gulfport to watch the submarine races. A time when we were in true fear for our lives—not because of home invasions, schoolyard drug dealers or random shootings from a speeding car; no, back then it was our parents who were the greater threat. But while they were a cause for real fear, we knew their love outweighed the peril. A time when we relied on "eeny-meeny-miney-moe" to make our decisions, and if we made a mistake, we simply yelled, "Do over!" A time when we were actually held back a grade if we failed in school. We weren't passed along just to protect our self-esteem. A time when we remember the smell of mimeograph paper, cleaning the erasers on the chalkboard after school, building houses with Lincoln Logs, collecting prizes in the bottoms of our cereal boxes, cutting out paper dolls, clamping our teeth on a set of wax lips, walking-the-dog with our rhinestone-encrusted Duncan Yo-Yos, shooting marbles, marking hopscotch on the sidewalk in colored chalk, trying to pick up a handful of Jacks with one bounce of the ball and attaching matchbook covers to the spokes of our bikes with clothespins to transform them into motorcycles. A time when all of the holidays were celebrated in school, even Christmas. Halloween was for ghosts and goblins, not fairytale princesses and American presidents' faces. A time when we could ride in the back of a pickup truck on a warm summer evening watching the trees go by and hearing the hum of the asphalt beneath the tires. We drank water from the garden hose, not from a bottle. We shared the hose with all of our friends, and I can't recall even one of us getting sick from it. We would spread real butter on white bread sprinkled with sugar and eat real cookies and cakes. No one was concerned about childhood obesity because we were always outside playing with our friends, riding our bikes, skating on the sidewalk, pushing our homemade go-carts or playing sandlot baseball.

It is easy for current generations to overlook the '50s. Compared to the high-tech, fast-action life of today, those years seem pretty much "dullsville." The decade of doo-wop and poodle skirts might seem like a boring time in America, but nothing could be further from the truth. There were many important events and discoveries that occurred during the '50s that have affected the world today. Life for us was far different from the images of that period that have been defined by ceaseless reruns of such overly sweet television shows as *Leave It to Beaver*, *Father Knows Best* and *The Donna Reed Show*. The pop media culture has presented an overly distorted view of the way things really were.

Growing Up in Gulfport is a look at the era in which the city and country prospered. And whether you are from the Mississippi Gulf Coast or not, anyone who grew up during the '50s and '60s can identify with these cultural norms that defined the era.

Chapter 1

REMEMBERING GULFPORT DURING THE GOLDEN AGE

*T*he Joseph W. Milner Stadium was dedicated on November 12, 1948. It was named for Milner, who was the Gulfport mayor for twenty-four years. Gulfport had only two mayors throughout all of the golden era. Mayor Milton T. "Mitt" Evans was sworn in on January 4, 1949. Mayor R.B. "Billy" Meadows Jr. took office on July 1, 1953, and served until 1969.

The four-lane Highway 90 (Beach Boulevard) through the city of Gulfport was opened on May 23, 1951.

Sears, Roebuck and Company opened a new store in Gulfport at the corner of 13th Street and 25th Avenue on May 22, 1952. It had the only escalator on the Gulf Coast.

Gulfport Memorial Hospital was built in 1953.

The four-lane, concrete and steel Bay St. Louis bridge opened on July 1, 1953. The old bridge it replaced was at that time the longest wooden bridge remaining in the world.

The Aluminum Plant opened in 1953.

The Glass Company opened next to the Phillips Milk of Magnesia plant in 1953.

The Air National Guard began training exercises at Gulfport Field in 1954. The thundering jets could be seen and heard as they flew over houses during practice runs.

The new B. Frank Brown Memorial Gymnasium was dedicated across the street from the Gulfport High School in 1955.

The Gulf National Bank opened its flagship bank at the intersection of 25th Avenue and Highway 90 in 1956.

St. John's Catholic Church built a new high school on Pass Road and Hewes Avenue in 1956.

Marine Life opened an aquarium in Jones Park in 1957.

The John C. Moses fishing pier opened in 1959.

Hardy Court Shopping Center opened in 1962, replacing the old Hardy Court apartments. The apartments had replaced Quonset huts used during World War II. The olive-green huts were made of corrugated galvanized steel.

The Gulf and Ship Island Building was completely renovated in 1962 with a new façade that covered up the grand old architecture in an attempt to modernize the building.

Gulfport East High School opened on September 4, 1966.

The new Gulfport–Harrison County Library building was dedicated on November 27, 1966.

Overall, there was a widespread sense of stability and contentment in Gulfport and throughout the country during the '50s. This was a time when most people believed in God and religion was respected. We said the Pledge of Allegiance to the flag with our hands over our hearts. We memorized the Gettysburg Address and learned to diagram a sentence. We learned real math and how to write in cursive. No one was asked to show an ID when cashing a check or when buying groceries at the market. In fact, we did not have a picture ID, not even on our driver's licenses. Many of us hitchhiked without fear.

Most of us in Gulfport lived in small, affordable houses. We didn't have cellphones or cable bills; we had only one telephone line, and we were careful with our long-distance calls because they were generally expensive. Since many housewives sewed for their families, store-bought dresses were for special occasions. We didn't know or care about designer clothing. Food was either fresh or canned, since very little frozen food was sold. The average income was less than $500 a month. There were no fancy power tools, so we cut our lawns with a push mower. Carpenters built our homes with a hammer and nails, not with a nail gun. Few of our families ever took vacations, but when they did, they were generally by car and most often to visit relatives. The only appliances in the kitchen were perhaps a toaster and a percolator for coffee. Most people in Gulfport cooled their homes with fans and used space heaters in each room for heat. Our mothers cooked nearly all of the meals and packed lunches for our fathers and the kids. Insurance premiums were low because no one sued over the least little thing. Fewer government regulations allowed Gulfport businesses to keep their costs down and not have to readjust to meet each new mandate. Products were not prepackaged, so there was no struggle to open shrink-wrapped plastic containers; we simply picked things off the shelf and took them home. Gasoline was cheaper, and we didn't use as much since we didn't have to commute. We generally worked in or around the area where we lived.

Nationally, there were only three major television networks, although in Gulfport we only received NBC from New Orleans and Mobile, so we all watched the same shows. People took care of their families and their neighbors. Those who had to rely on welfare and other government assistance did so reluctantly and got back on their feet as quickly as possible. Marriage

Downtown Gulfport, 1956. *Clayton Rand Papers, Manuscripts Division, Special Collections Department, Mississippi State University Libraries.*

was sacred. The divorce rate was less than half of today's rate. Illegitimate births were only about 3 percent and were not celebrated as the standard. For the first time in history, the normal American family was fashioned, not by reality, but by the images projected on television, in magazines and on the backs of cereal boxes.

There was a dichotomy of style. Like in the rest of the country, we were obsessed with rockets and rocket shapes, but we were equally obsessed with early America and the pioneers. The contrast between the two styles was evident in Gulfport homes. The kitchens were often futuristic with state-of-the-art appliances, while the living room or the dining room was decorated with early American furniture and accessories. Even the newly opened Disneyland gave us a choice between Frontierland on the one hand and Tomorrowland on the other.

Although the predominant trend in the country was toward a futuristic look, the look of motion and speed was offset by an impression of homey, family-style togetherness. Television shows like *The Andy Griffith Show* and *The Donna Reed Show* presented an ideal image of family life.

Some of our parents told us that comic books were a bad influence on young children, that the raucous new music called rock 'n' roll was evil and that watching television dumbed down our minds. Many parents even banned their children from going to the Gulf Theatre across from the L&N depot. They saw it as a rat-infested haven for derelicts and riffraff.

Comic books in particular seemed to be the object of a national witch hunt, as they were blamed for the disturbing rise in juvenile delinquency. In 1964, William Gaines, the publisher of *Mad* magazine, was called to testify about his controversial comic books that included *Tales from the Crypt*, *The Vault of Horror*, *Shock Suspense Stories*, *Weird Science* and *Two-Fisted Tales*. Gaines argued that while they may be objectionable to some, they were completely acceptable within the horror comic genre.

In reality, Entertaining Comics, better known as EC comics, was not just a group of morbid stories illustrated with extremely gory pictures. Many dealt with adult issues and, aside from the gruesome images, were well-crafted tales. As a result of the subcommittee, however, many comics, including EC, were forced to alter their contents or cease publishing altogether.

The growing interest in popular psychology seemed to encourage young mothers to ignore the advice of their parents as being outdated and irrelevant in the modern times. Many Gulfport mothers put their faith in the popular child-rearing manual *Baby and Child Care* by Dr. Benjamin Spock rather than seeking direction from their own parents.

This growing look to psychology did not go unnoticed by the advertisers, who used psychological techniques to give additional weight to their products. In 1957, a widely popular book, *The Hidden Persuaders*, by author Vance Packard, stunned the public by exposing the mental manipulations used in some advertising. Today, we recognize many of these methods as being blatantly obvious. In 1955, Camel cigarettes touted, "It's a psychological fact: Pleasure helps your disposition." Another ad depicting a physician smoking a cigarette read, "More doctors smoke Camels than any other cigarette."

The right combination of low taxes, balanced budgets and consumer spending allowed the Gulfport economy to flourish. Leading the way was the domestic production of cheap oil. In Gulfport and along the coast, gas was eighteen cents a gallon in 1950, and by 1959, it had only risen to twenty-five cents.

In addition to low gasoline prices, the Federal Housing Administration introduced low-interest-rate loans. This, along with the new GI Bill, caused a dramatic increase in home purchases. The government also gave military veterans easy access to affordable college loans. Having a college degree was becoming more important for a successful career.

Along with this new prosperity, however, there was an underlying fear in Gulfport of another war. In 1952, the United States tested the first super bomb, now called a hydrogen bomb, which was one thousand times more powerful than the atomic bombs dropped on Hiroshima and Nagasaki, Japan. Shortly after, the Russians tested one of their own. Throughout the '50s, the two countries, along with the French and the British, continued to test and develop more sophisticated bombs.

In 1961, President John F. Kennedy warned against the possibility of a nuclear attack and urged all Americans to build bomb shelters in their yards to protect themselves against atomic fallout in the event of a confrontation with the Soviets. Although the bomb shelter craze did not heat up so much in Gulfport and along the coast, a craze for fallout shelters developed in other parts of the country.

We were understandably anxious, as we were continually being told that communists were infiltrating our country. In the early 1950s, Senator Joseph McCarthy was accusing some of our most respected citizens of being communists, and we were glued to our television sets each week to watch the popular show *I Led Three Lives*, starring actor Richard Carlson. The program kept us enthralled with the exploits of Herbert Philbrick, a Boston advertising executive who had infiltrated the U.S. Communist

Party at the request of the FBI. The program was a real-life dramatization loosely based on Philbrick's bestselling book, *I Led Three Lives: Citizen, Communist, Counterspy*. With such emphasis on communist takeover, it is no wonder we had reason to fear.

The fear became real in October 1957 when the United States was stunned to learn that Russia had launched the first man-made satellite into space. This basketball-sized sphere called Sputnik was science fiction come true. Movies like *This Island Earth, The Day the Earth Stood Still* and *It Came from Outer Space* depicted a futuristic world that seemed to suddenly be a real possibility. Not only was the country shocked at losing our lead in space technology, but we were also angered when the Russians launched an even larger satellite less than a month after Sputnik. This time, the Soviet satellite carried a live dog into space. Unbelievable!

Public hysteria went through the roof when the United States finally tried to launch our own three-pound satellite several months later. On December 3, 1957, the navy was set to launch its Vanguard rocket, which was supposed to propel the first U.S. satellite into space. The nation was stunned as the rocket literally disintegrated on the launch pad. The newspaper headlines were not kind as they mocked the launch, calling the failed rocket "Flopnik" and "Kaputnik," among other critical labels. It seemed the country was even further behind the Russians than any of us could have ever imagined.

In Gulfport, our anxiety over the possibility of nuclear war contrasted with our feelings of complacency. This dichotomy of fear and contentment caused a whole new phenomenon not yet seen in the country. The uneasiness that many of us felt led to the increased use of tranquilizers. A personal search for reassurance resulted in the nation's turn to religion and individual counseling.

One successful minister who merged a generic public religion with a growing psychological self-help movement was the Reverend Norman Vincent Peale. In 1952, Peale's popular book, *The Power of Positive Thinking*, promoted the idea that with faith and self-confidence, anyone could overcome life's many problems.

While the turn to faith was seen in all of the mainstream denominations, there was a resurgence of evangelical Christianity. The major spokesman was the late Reverend Billy Graham, who viewed the increasing emphasis on materialism in the world as an encroaching evil. His followers were more interested in cleansing themselves from sin than improving themselves through "positive thinking."

Brother Byron Jessup was an evangelist with local ties on the Mississippi Gulf Coast. Born in Gulfport in 1929, he preferred to be called "Brother" rather than "Reverend." Jessup and his seven brothers traveled the country with their father, who was also a minister, performing and preaching at various revivals. The people of Gulfport could hear Brother Jessup on WGCM radio for many years.

On the social front, the tensions over race and civil rights issues were growing. Gulfport was the focus of civil unrest in 1958, when the media reported that Clennon Washington King Jr., a history professor at Alcorn State University, was going to have one of his children try to integrate an all-white elementary school in the city. North Central Ward School, located on the Pass Road between 20th and 21st Avenues, was alerted as the possible target, but King's wife and children fled before any actual attempt was made.

During the golden age of Gulfport, there were also dramatic advances in modern medicine. In 1955, Dr. Jonas Salk created a vaccine for the prevention of polio. Until the Salk vaccine, there was no effective method of treatment. In addition to the polio vaccine, the first tranquilizers were introduced. These drugs fit perfectly in a culture that was beginning to seek

The new Broadwater Beach Hotel.

The Hotel Markham. *Paul Jermyn collection.*

emotional and psychological assurances. The popularity of pills such as Miltown and Equinil led to a surge in the future development of mind-altering drugs. In other developments, antihistamines were created to control the effects of allergies, giving many Gulfport sufferers relief from itchy eyes and scratchy throats.

With the success of the first electronic computer, called ENIAC, the 1950s ushered in the era of computers. ENIAC, built in secret in 1943 at the University of Pennsylvania, required thousands of vacuum tubes to run and used so much electricity it was said that the lights in Philadelphia would dim when the machine was turned on. It was little more than a glorified calculator, only capable of multiplying up to a maximum of ten digits. Although it was considered a success, it could only run for a short time before some of the many vacuum tubes would burn out and need replacing.

The world's first commercially produced transistor radio was introduced in 1954 and quickly became a universal success. The growing popularity of rock 'n' roll music and the increase in disposable income due to the prosperous economy drove the sale of these pocket-sized radios.

In 1950, tourists from the North were discovering the warm, balmy atmosphere of the coast and were coming to the area in droves to escape

Bayou View, Gulfport's first subdivision, was developed from areas in Gulfport Field. *Paul Jermyn collection.*

the northern cold. Many tourist cottages and nightclubs were beginning to spring up, bringing in such big-name entertainment as Hank Williams, Andy Griffith and Jayne Mansfield. Large hotels like the Great Southern, the Buena Vista, the Edgewater Gulf and the Hotel Markham offered first-class accommodations. Mrs. Joe W. Brown, whose husband bought the old Broadwater Beach Hotel, transformed the aging Art Deco property into the coast's most luxurious resort. The construction of the three-hundred-foot-wide sand beach along with the simultaneous widening of Highway 90 made the area even more attractive for the snowbirds wanting to escape the cold.

Bayou View, the first real subdivision in Gulfport, was developed from areas in the old World War II Gulfport Air Field, while the wartime airport was upgraded to the city's main terminal. In addition, the National Guard training facility at the airport was completed.

In 1962, WLOX-TV, the Gulf Coast's first television station, opened in the Buena Vista Hotel, and in the following year, Edgewater Mall, the coast's first regional shopping mall, was opened on forty acres of the property belonging to the old Edgewater Gulf Hotel.

During the late '40s and early '50s, the population that had declined as a result of the Depression in the '30s was experiencing an explosion. Postwar births went up dramatically as soldiers returned home to their families. This large rise in the number of children being born led to the term "baby boomer." The word "boom" was one of the catchwords used to describe much of this period. It was applied to the "booming economy," the "booming suburbs" and the "baby boom," which is counted from 1946 and until 1964.

During Gulfport's golden age, our generation had the freedom to make our own success, to be responsible for our own actions and, yes, even to face our own failures. But from it all, we grew stronger. The freedoms that we knew produced some of the best risk-takers, problem solvers and inventors the world has ever known.

Chapter 2

OUR HOUSES IN THE '50s

The Servicemen's Readjustment Act of 1944, known as the GI Bill, dramatically increased homeownership in Gulfport after World War II. The bill created low-interest mortgages to help returning veterans buy homes. In addition, it allowed servicemen to get a college or trade school education by covering their tuition and expenses.

With a pressing need for houses, Gulfport home builders were forced to seek innovative ways to meet these demands at a reasonable cost. One solution was the repetitive use of house plans to build reasonably priced homes in the same way that automobile manufacturers used mass production to provide affordable cars. This "cookie cutter" approach made homes affordable for buyers and profitable for builders. Developers used basic plans that could be personalized by choosing various options and add-ons to give their houses the appearance of being different.

In Gulfport, the Bayou View subdivision was perfect for this new approach to housing. In 1947, the U.S. government that had used the airfield during the war for military purposes turned the site over to the city for use as a commercial airport. This was the second Gulfport Airport. The first had opened in 1930 on a 165-acre tract on the north side of 28th Street, across from the Mac Smith Garment Factory. In 1950, Gulfport turned its attention to Gulfport Field as a reasonable answer to the housing needs of the city. The area between Pass Road and Bayou Bernard, with the exception of the land used for the new municipal airport, was designated as the Bayou View subdivision. The new subdivision was planned to include seven hundred residential lots, along with retail shops, commercial businesses, parks, schools and play areas. In the beginning, small box-type houses sprang up all along Washington Avenue. They were not characteristic of the upscale houses that Bayou View would later be known for.

New colors and new color combinations in the auto industry and in fashion characterized every aspect of the '50s, including our houses. Great new colors were offered to liven up the previously boring rooms. *House Beautiful* magazine even stated, "One color alone is next to nothing." Other decorating magazines brought attention to this new craze with articles on "this year's colors." Color charts were developed, helping buyers put together color combinations that expressed their own styles. The colors were crisp and different from the colors that were typically derived from nature. If there was a preference for any one color, the use of turquoise seemed to be pronounced throughout the mid-century. The marked interest in new colors meant that houses were painted more often to keep up with the trends.

Familiar appliances were upgraded with new features, while new models were added. Machines took on a boxier look and were often adorned with decorative appliques. Appliances followed the automobile companies' lead by introducing new colors to machines that had always been white. The addition of fashionable colors, such as avocado, mustard and coral, made the appliances seem dated in a very short time. And while popular two-tone color combinations became a trend in the automotive industry, two-color appliances never caught on.

Single-story ranch-style houses became the fashion in Gulfport, although builders included elements of both traditional and contemporary designs in each of their different kinds of houses. Many felt that contemporary alone was too cold without some of the traditional features. Likewise, traditional houses were too stuffy and needed a touch of the contemporary.

In Gulfport, the influence of the southern plantations was evident. Many of the ranch-style houses in Bayou View and other parts of the coast featured large entryways with white four-by-fours replacing the classic columns.

The most defining feature of the Gulfport suburban houses was the picture window. The window was created as a design element to break up the basic boxy look and to make the small postwar-era houses seem larger. The picture window became so popular that it was ultimately used in just about every style of house built during that period. Even some of the more expensive houses featured a picture window. They were even added to older houses to give the appearance that the house had been updated. It also added light to the interior. Since first impressions count, eye-catching trees, shrubs and flowering plants were added in the front of the house. The large glass window allowed the owner to look out and enjoy his front yard. Since the picture window was also a view into the house from the outside, it became important to consider what was seen when looking at the house. Often a decorative table lamp, a colorful plant or some other interesting item was placed in the window.

A black ornamental lamppost in the front yard was another familiar item in Gulfport homes. The flickering gaslight was a welcoming touch. As the appearance of the yard became increasingly important, many neighborhoods began to feature a "lawn of the month." It was enough of a status that some residents actively tried to win this award.

In Gulfport, one-story houses were preferred, but because of increasing cost concerns, developers wanted to build two-story houses to offer more space on small lots. This difference led to split-level houses that presented a compromise between one- and two-story houses. In 1954, no one had

The picture window was the most defining feature of the home.

ever heard of a split-level house, but in 1955, it became the universally accepted design, lasting well into the '60s. The new design made it easier for the homeowner to walk up a few steps rather than a whole flight of stairs, and it allowed the builders to save on construction costs. Split-level houses have long since gone out of style, but some can still be found in the suburbs today.

In the late '50s, floor plans became more open. Living rooms and dining rooms were combined into one large space. Kitchens were combined with breakfast areas so that many ate their meals at the kitchen table. New furniture was developed to serve as room dividers. Storage units called étagères were used to delineate the areas into the impression of rooms. In some cases, bar-type counters replaced walls that separated kitchens and dens.

New kinds of rooms emerged in the '50s, the most significant being the "family room." The family room began as a playroom, but by mid-century, as the use of the formal living room declined, it developed into the most popular living area in the house. By 1960, the television had been moved to the family room. Cozy elements such as a brick fireplace, wood paneling and more durable and comfortable furniture were common. The living room was commonly decorated with traditional furniture and was now used for formal entertaining, if it were used at all.

With the growing popularity of the family room and an increase in the size of families, there was a need for sturdier furniture that could withstand the constant and rugged use by overactive children, lounging parents and TV watchers who spent most of their time in this room. To accommodate this need, U.S. Rubber developed an imitation leather called Naugahyde. Naugahyde was extremely durable and safe and could hold up to even the most active family. The authentic leather look appealed to middle-class Americans, who were striving to improve their lifestyles. In addition, Naugahyde was available in the latest colors, which made it perfect for just about any décor.

Houses in Gulfport were far different from the ones today. Many of our homes in the mid-'50s contained less than 1,000 square feet of living space. Today, our houses have morphed into McMansions, some of which have as much as 7,500 square feet. Most of our houses in the '50s had only one bathroom, whereas today, there is a bath for every bedroom plus at least one powder room, or half bath. The rooms are now much larger; even the closets are room size. Bathrooms in the '50s were more functional than luxurious. The once cramped space is now a well-appointed area with separate tub and shower and a separate his and hers lavatory.

Since the '50s, the kitchen has become a center of social activity. In the past, housewives were secluded in their isolated kitchens, while friends and family enjoyed themselves in the living room or den. Architects in the '70s began to tear down walls, extending the kitchen into the family room and encouraging people to mingle while the food was being prepared. The once dark room was brightened by the addition of skylights and larger windows. A bar, where snacks and light meals were sometimes served, often separated the kitchen from the living area.

In the '50s, Gulfport families ate their meals together at the dining room table. This allowed parents and children to have quality time to discuss concerns of the day. Today's busy families hardly eat together, causing a formal dining room to become obsolete. Now, families prefer to eat in the kitchen, partially because of the convenience of carrying dishes to the table and the ease of cleaning up after.

Chapter 3

NEW PRODUCTS INTRODUCED

*A*lthough it was a time of much social conformity, in many ways the era was a true contradiction. Americans seemed to be obsessed with the future, as can be seen by the "swept-wing styling" and "the forward look" of many products, most notably our cars.

The influence of the jet plane could also be seen on many products as we were becoming aware that we were living in the jet age. Not only did the airplane represent speed, but it was also a symbol of the growing change in national attitudes, which was happening faster than ever before. Even commercial buildings were designed to lean slightly forward in the same sweeping design of the cars. Other than a small variation, such as an overhanging roof or a slight addition here and there, most of the buildings were more or less the same. In order to stand out, features such as McDonald's golden arches and the sweeping canopy at the entrance of the newly redesigned Broadwater Beach Hotel were added to transform an otherwise ordinary building into something quite memorable.

The two most characteristic designs of the '50s were the boomerang and the starburst. These could be found on fabric, wallpaper, furniture, signs, corporate logos and just about everything else. The boomerang suggested the forward thrust of the space age. In 1955, Chrysler incorporated the boomerang into its logo to symbolize the "forward look." The boomerang shape is still popular today on such corporate logos as Nike.

The furniture tended to be modern in design, employing the boomerang or parabolic shape on just about everything. One of the most widespread

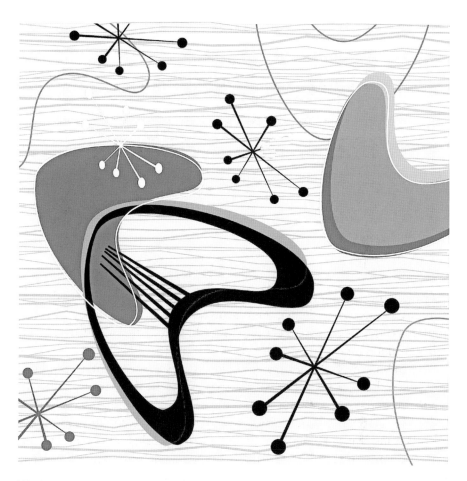

The boomerang and starburst were the most characteristic designs of the '50s.

and identifiable pieces of furniture was the Hardoy butterfly chair. The chair was featured in many magazine ads and in movies to exemplify a modern setting. The chair looked like four large paperclips supporting a colorful sling that formed the seat and back.

The increase in manufacturing also allowed us to buy new and better things. There were new industries developing, most notably in the fields of electronics and aviation. Manufacturers introduced a wide variety of new products for the home, but not all were successful. The automatic washing machine and, a few years later, the clothes dryer were readily accepted. The new washer had replaced the labor-intensive wringer type that our mothers thought was a modern convenience at the time. While the washer and dryer were big successes, items such as the freestanding deep freeze were failures. At first the new freezer was very popular, but after buyers struggled with the rock-hard stacks of food and the solid chunks of ice that would form, the freezers virtually disappeared from the stores. Freezers eventually made a comeback, but this time as a larger section of the regular refrigerator.

Another surprising failure at first was the electric dishwasher. It wasn't until manufacturers began to include them as permanent built-ins that the dishwasher became accepted.

The Hardoy butterfly chair.

To keep up with the volume of consumer demands, handmade items were no longer practical. Products made by machines became the norm. These machine-made items were in many ways inferior to the hand-crafted products of the past. People understood that the items were mass-produced, but they didn't really seem to care. Although the quality was missing, manufacturers were able to reproduce an acceptable likeness of fine furniture and antiques. This allowed the consumer to enjoy the look and feeling of elegance that had previously only been available to the wealthy. We knew we were purchasing fakes, but that was okay.

Durability was no longer the focus. Nearly all of the products were purchased knowing that something newer would soon be available. These newer products were not necessarily better and in many cases were basically the same. The changes were often just cosmetic to give the appearance of being upgraded. A television set might be advertised as new and improved when actually nothing changed but the position of the knobs that might have been moved from the bottom of the set to the top. Cars were sold as luxury autos by simply adding new carpet and some chrome strips to the basic models. Although most of us realized the difference, we were still willing to go for the prestige of owning the pricier models. After the new Thunderbird came out, Ford ran advertisements touting its other models as having "Thunderbird styling." That was just marketing hype that was selling a fantasy, since the style of the cars had nothing to do with the style of the Thunderbird.

Families understood that everything was replaceable. Planned obsolescence was a concept promoted by General Motors since the 1920s. With machine-made goods being accepted as the norm, things were specifically designed not to last. The widespread increase in disposable income led to a disposable society. "Use it once and throw it out" had become a marketing promotion for many of the new products. Whether something wore out or not, we always had in mind that we could move up to something better. The durability of the product was not the important point, but rather production, sales and continuing economic activity were the goals. It was change or the impression of change that induced consumers to buy.

At General Electric, the focus was on selling the idea of progress, not on selling products, because they couldn't keep coming up with new light bulbs every year. GE focused on developing small appliances instead. GE products included the electric frying pan, the four-slice toaster, the spray-steam-and-dry iron, the electric can opener and other convenient items.

The most important new design element was not a pattern, shape or color but rather a physical feature: the handle. We were becoming a mobile society, and the idea of being able to move things around the house was very appealing. When added to a piece of furniture or appliance, a handle gave the suggestion of portability even if it was useless. The large pre-transistor picture tubes made television sets too heavy to be moved on a practical basis. TV stands became common to hold the portable televisions so they could be rolled from one room to the next.

One of the most innovative products from the mid-1950s was Tupperware. These airtight containers were not decorated with boomerangs and starbursts but instead were plain but efficient. With the advent of frost-free refrigerators, the Tupperware bowls protected chilled food in refrigerators from dehydration and freezer burn. The success of Tupperware was the result of a brilliant marketing scheme: the home Tupperware parties. The hostess would invite her friends and neighbors over to her house to demonstrate and hopefully take orders for the products. The company would reward the hostess with a gift based on the amount of sales made during the party. Each of the ladies who attended also received a gift.

Throughout the '50s, the term "push button" invoked an image of cutting-edge technology. The use of push buttons on just about every product of that period didn't do anything to improve performance. The buttons had merely replaced the rotary dial, giving only the appearance of being high-tech. Push buttons showed up on stoves, blenders, washing machines and even automobiles. The most famous was the Edsel, which featured push buttons on the steering wheel to replace the standard gearshift lever. There were so many buttons on a blender that it was confusing which button to press. Some of the buttons seemed useless. After all, "liquefy" and "puree" are pretty much the same thing.

The underlying element with push buttons went beyond convenience. Once the button was pressed, the appliance was on its own, regardless of what you did from that point forward. Hotpoint even declared, "All you do is press the button to start the washer, it does the rest."

In Gulfport and throughout the nation, there was a dramatic increase in consumer spending. This increased spending was partially due to the introduction of easy credit. Our parents, who had lived through the Depression, were very cautious with their spending. But the children of Gulfport's golden age were now turning away from their parents' inclination toward thrift. This led to the widespread use of credit.

New offerings of loans and credit by the banks and credit companies like Gulfport's Household Finance Corporation gave us the perception of personal success by allowing us to get what we wanted immediately. Manufacturers encouraged this new trend. In a typical magazine ad, Chevrolet prompted its customers to "Buy Now, Pay Later."

A dramatic growth in borrowing resulted from the new easy money that banks and credit companies were beginning to offer. People borrowed to buy everything from automobiles to appliances and even larger houses. It now seemed like there was nothing we could not have, as our personal debt skyrocketed. This extravagant use of credit not only boosted the economy but also allowed many to enjoy the good things in life that had been out of their reach in the past.

In 1951, the Diners Club issued the first ever credit card. Even though only a limited number of restaurants accepted the card at first, the concept of paying with plastic took off. In 1958, American Express and the Bank Americard, which later became VISA, were introduced.

All over the country, including Gulfport and the Mississippi Gulf Coast, we were changing from a production society to a consumption society. We were no longer focused on just meeting our needs; we were now much more interested in satisfying our wants. This new affluence allowed us to turn our attention to more stylish and trendy items. In the past, our parents had been forced not only to save but also to reuse. Now, people wanted everything new and felt no remorse about throwing things away.

Television, along with other cultural factors, promoted our feelings of a better life. Robert Sarnoff, the president of NBC, nailed it in 1956 when he said, "The reason we have such a high standard of living is because advertising has created an American frame of mind that makes people want more things, better things, and newer things."

There were so many new products available, although the average shopper in Gulfport rarely ever purchased fine things. What they often bought was fun. For the first time, common objects took on a novel and unique style, available in a wide variety of colors that had never been used before. Kitchen appliances and bathroom fixtures that were always white in the past were now appearing in avocado, mustard and even pink. These novel designs became so universal that they were quickly accepted as commonplace.

The abundance of new things to buy seemed endless. Instead of cutting our grass with a push mower, we were now cranking up a gasoline engine to do the same job. The old wringer-style washing machine that we once thought was an innovative improvement over our grandparents' scrubbing boards was now replaced by front-loading automatic washers with a window through which we could stand transfixed, watching the soap suds as they turned the water to gray.

Women were depicted in magazine ads in unrealistic situations. Although they were always stylishly dressed, the clothing was often impractical. The lady of the house might be shown wearing gloves to press the button on her latest kitchen appliance. The women were never shown on their hands and knees scrubbing the floor, unless it was to show a time before modern cleansers and labor-saving devices.

We were all connected as never before through advertising, television and slick magazines. We had become a unified "mass market" that manufacturers quickly recognized to be a powerful generator of profits and economic growth.

The postwar baby boom did not go unnoticed by the manufacturers, which recognized how much of an economic powerhouse children could be. In 1954, Dr. Frances Horwitch, Miss Frances of television's *Ding Dong School*, told advertisers, "Never underestimate the buying power of a child under seven." She pointed out that they had brand loyalty and the determination to demand their favorite cereal, snacks and toys.

In addition to the appliances and various items for the kitchen, there were other products from food to cars and everything in between. A random sampling of new products includes Con-Tact paper, Saran Wrap, stereo recordings, synthetic fabric, 45 rpm records, TV dinners, power steering, Crest toothpaste, Kleenex tissue, diet soda, roll-on deodorant, Scotchgard, Liquid Paper and Velcro.

Chapter 4

COMING OF AGE IN THE '50s

*C*hildren in Gulfport during the '50s were truly blessed. Expectations were much higher for the children who grew up in the '30s and '40s. Before our generation, there was no recognized in-between age. The term "teenager" had not been used before the '50s. Young people were supposed to act like young adults.

During the '30s and '40s, it was common for teenagers to work full-time jobs to help support their families. But by the time we reached our teens, very few, if any, of us had to work full time. In addition, many of us also received a small allowance from our parents, for which we were usually expected to perform certain household chores. For the most part, the money we earned was our money, and for the first time, we were able to spend it on ourselves on fun nonessential items like cars, clothes and records.

As the economy flourished, and with less responsibilities and more free time, we began to see ourselves as a distinct group. We had our own discretionary cash, and we were beginning to develop our own styles. Our attempt to create an individual identity worried our parents, who couldn't understand what was happening.

Until the '50s, teenagers had been mostly ignored. There was nothing that spoke to us directly. There was nothing on the radio aimed at our age group. It wasn't until the introduction of rock 'n' roll during the mid-'50s that we began to come into our own.

Without the cultural impact of the music—our music—the '50s would hardly be worth mentioning. The '50s music that now seems so innocent was in fact a subversive force that alienated our parents and unleashed an unprecedented revolution. To the adults, rock 'n' roll was the devil's music with threatening lyrics delivered by pelvis-thrusting singers like Elvis Presley and black performers like Chuck Berry, Fats Domino and Little Richard. But what they didn't understand was that the music touched our core. It was our music, and only ours, and it couldn't be stopped.

For the first time, we were hearing music about "our" world, sung by other teenagers, not stodgy old crooners of our parents' day. Our songs were about high school sweethearts, teenage romance, wild parties and fast cars. We began developing into our own distinct subculture. Now we were becoming increasingly unlike what our parents had known.

As these differences continued to grow, the resistance to these changes caused some of us to question our parents and in some ways lose a little respect for society as a whole. Strict rules were put in place. Rock 'n' roll records were often banned, and some teen dances were cancelled or heavily chaperoned. The music was attacked as causing juvenile delinquency. Alan Freed, the DJ who gave rock 'n' roll its name, was personally and professionally destroyed by a government corruption investigation.

The growing desire among many to put space between our parents' generation and us was reflected in our language, as new words were introduced and old words took on new meanings. Our new expressions covered everything, including dating, music, people and certain conditions or events. Over time, some of this slang was used so universally that it has transitioned into our regular language and is still in use today.

Some of the more common slang expressions that were popular in Gulfport and throughout the country in the '50s were:

Bad news: depressing person
Bash: great party
Blast: a good time
Bread: money
Bug ("you bug me"): to bother
Burn rubber: to accelerate hard and fast (hot-rodders)
Cat: a hip person
Closet case: someone to be ashamed of
Cloud 9: really happy
Cool: indefinable quality that makes something or someone extraordinary
Cool it: relax, settle down
Corrode: to feel embarrassed about something

Crazy ("like crazy, man"): implies an especially good thing

Cream: originally, to dent a car; later, to badly damage anything

Cruisin' for a bruisin': looking for trouble

Cut out: leave

Dibs: a claim, as in "got dibs" on that seat

Dig: to understand; to approve

Far out: ahead of the times

Flat out: fast as you can

Flick: a movie

Flip: to get very excited

Floor it: push the accelerator to the floor (hot-rodders)

Gig: work, job

Go ape: to explode or be really mad; to get very excited

Goof: someone who makes mistakes; to make a mistake

Hang ("hang out"): to do very little; to loaf or idle

Hip: someone who is cool, in the know; very good; up to date and informed

I'll clue you: I'll tell you about it

Kooky: nuts, in the nicest possible way

Made in the shade: success guaranteed

Make the scene: to attend an event or activity

Mickey Mouse: dumb

Nerd: same as now—Bill Gates without the money

No sweat: no problem

Nowheresville: a boring, bad place to be

Pad: home; an apartment

Party pooper: no fun at all; a killjoy

Passion pit: drive-in movie theater

Pop the clutch: release the clutch pedal quickly so as to get a fast start

Punk: a weak, useless person

Rag top: a convertible car

Rattle your cage: get upset

Raunchy: messy or gross in some other way

Snowed: infatuated

Souped up: a car modified to go fast

Spaz: someone who is uncoordinated; a klutz

Split: leave

Square: a regular, normal person; a conformist

Threads: clothes

Other words and expressions have become virtually obsolete. When was the last time you heard these?

Don't take any wooden nickels.
Gee whillikers!
Heavens to Betsy!
Holy moley!
Hunky dory
I'll be a monkey's uncle!
I'll see you in the funny papers.
In like Flynn.
Jalopy
Knee high to a grasshopper.
Knucklehead
Nincompoop
Not for all the tea in China!
Oh, my aching back!
Okey-dokey!
See ya later, alligator! After a while, crocodile!
Well, Fiddlesticks!

A generation gap was widening, as we were viewed to be rebellious. Our sense of separation from the mainstream increased as teenage movies like *Don't Knock the Rock, High School Confidential* and *Rock, Rock, Rock* expressed the upheaval that we were beginning to feel. James Dean, the star of *Rebel Without a Cause,* and Marlon Brando, star of *The Wild One,* became leading symbols of teenagers who were lost, unhappy and lacking direction. In truth, the movie title was correct: we did not have a cause. We never intended to start a revolution or seek societal reform. We were just pursuing our lives in different ways than our parents understood.

Juvenile delinquency was a big topic in the '50s. The rapidly growing numbers of teenagers accompanied by the wide coverage in the media made the problem seem much worse than it was. Of course, delinquency in the '50s didn't mean dealing drugs or shooting people in the street like it does today, but rather was usually nothing more sinister than talking back to our teachers or drag racing on the streets.

Although gangs were not prevalent in Gulfport, a few of us were drawn to the look of these rebels, if not their behavior. Some adopted the leather jackets, motorcycle boots and ducktail hairstyle made popular in *The*

Blackboard Jungle. But those who did so were hardly rebellious and almost never broke the law.

To some extent, the GIs returning from World War II seemed to have a strong influence on the way we acted. Our generation tended to imitate the defiant, rebellious pattern of this older group, including the hairstyle. The short GI haircut that allowed only one and a half inches in length max became the dominant style in Gulfport for more than twenty years. In the '50s, the flattop emerged as a trendy variation of the GI cut, although not every boy's hair could be made to stand up so perfectly because of cowlicks and curls. Gerald Holmes of Holmes Barber Shop in Gulfport was the premier barber for students and teenagers. Only Holmes had the special talent to give the classic flattop cut—at least that is what most of his teenage patrons thought.

Through much of the '50s, Gulfport boys stuck to their flattops. Elvis, however, proved to have such an irresistible appeal to thousands of teenage girls that the boys began to let their flattops grow out. By brushing the long hair back on the sides, growing sideburns and allowing a well-oiled curl of hair to dangle in the center of the forehead, the ducktail-style hairdo emerged.

Boys who took on the defiant look tried to copy the black leather jacket of Marlon Brando and the coolness of James Dean. In addition to the ducktail haircuts, they wore white T-shirts with one sleeve rolled up to hold a pack of Lucky Strike cigarettes, tapered black pants and black shoes or preferably black motorcycle boots.

Despite what some of our parents feared, our rebellion was not about society. We were not concerned with social problems. Our conflicts were with our parents and the restrictions they imposed. We were, in fact, described as the "silent generation" because we were not activists like the generation of the '60s. It is true that our changing attitudes seemed to be of some concern, but as we grew up, we fell back into the norms of society. Almost half of us were drafted and served our time in the military with little resistance. Even Elvis Presley, the icon of defiant youth, respectfully served his time in the army.

By the mid-'50s, we began to develop a growing desire for anything new, and that included the clothes we wore. Compared to prior teens, we had a huge spending power that allowed us to make carefree purchases. Well aware of our extra cash, we became the target of manufacturers and advertisers that moved away from the middle-aged and senior groups as the prime focus of their attention. We became a marketing goldmine.

The previous generation had been very conservative, but we changed all of that. There was a trend to bolder fashions. With bigger dresses and taller hairstyles, shoes were simple and understated. Gulfport girls wore basic flats, pumps and loafers, while men's fashion was all about short haircuts, narrow suits and plaid or khaki pants.

Our music influenced fashion, as the dances required less restrictive clothing. A more lighthearted sense of life led to such items as the poodle skirt, which made it much easier to dance along with the beat. The skirts were the perfect length—just below the knee—to kick and jive. The felt material came in a variety of colors, with the image of a poodle dog appliqued on one side for accent. A sweater along with bobby socks and saddle oxfords completed the look.

When we started going to dances, the guys wore what was probably their first suits, usually gray flannel, most likely purchased at M. Salloum's. White, pink or blue oxford cloth with button-down collars were a must have. It was important that the brand was Gant.

At first, our neckties were narrow with a subtle stripe, but by the late '50s, ties had gotten wider to match a trend of wider lapels for suits and sport coats. The most popular pattern became wide military stripes in black and red, blue and gold or some similar contrasting combination. For proms, white sport coats were fashionable, as noted in the Marty Robbins song "A White Sport Coat and Pink Carnation."

When we headed off to college, we were wearing khakis with solid leather belts about an inch wide and usually brown. Gant shirts were still a must have, along with loafers, bucks and wingtips. Elmer's Oxford Shop and Salloum's The Toggery were the stores of choice to find the proper brands. We also wore letter sweaters and only wore leather if it was part of a team jacket.

Full skirts were the rage. Since the full skirts needed lots of support, petticoats were not only popular but also necessary. On top, the girls wore scoop-neck blouses or tight polo necks with back to front cardigans. Sometimes they would wear three-quarter sleeve white shirts with a scarf knotted at the side of the neck.

Full skirts were not restricted to casual wear, however; the prom dresses that were common at the cotillion balls and other formal dances on the coast were light tulle gowns with lots of stiff crinoline underneath with tight strapless bodices on top.

Sweaters were popular, whether they were Banlon with three buttons left undone or Shetland cardigans buttoned up the back. For a dressier

M. Salloum's Toggery, 1959. *Clayton Rand Papers, Manuscripts Division, Special Collections Department, Mississippi State University Libraries.*

look, the girls wore fuzzy sweaters decorated with rhinestones, sequins or beads.

For casual wear, girls wore jeans with loafers and bobby socks. In the later '50s, the fad was to cut off the jeans and fray the edges. Bermuda shorts, either plain colored or plaid, were very popular for both boys and girls. Later, Jamaica shorts were popular, which were the same as Bermudas only shorter. Also popular were pedal pushers, capris and clam diggers; pleated skirts; car coats; madras shirts; rope belts; circle pins; skorts (an early version of culottes); boat-necked sweaters; cummerbunds; colored tights; clutch purses; and sheaths.

The sheath look was popular for several years. It was characterized by a long, cylindrical profile that tapered in the middle. The shape was so much a part of the '50s that it transcended fashion and became known as "modern elegance." The sleek lines could be seen on other objects as diverse as the handle of a Frigidaire, the legs of Danish modern furniture and consumer products like Futurama lipstick by Revlon.

One dress style that came and went quickly after much ridicule was the chemise dress. Men hated it, and I think women hated it even more. Although it was called a chemise by the fashion industry, everyone else called it a sack dress. It consisted of a tube of material that ballooned out in the middle. In an attempt to improve the look, some women tried cinching it at the waist with a wide belt or gathering it in the back and attaching a large bow, but nothing helped. Pop singer Gerry Granahan's hit record from 1958 said it all: "No Chemise Please."

Living on the Gulf Coast meant a lot of time spent on the beach or at pools like those at the Hotel Markham, the Broadwater or the Sun 'n Sand. Bikinis were not yet popular in Gulfport, but girls were beginning to wear two-piece bathing suits. These suits were not as risqué as later bikinis. The bottoms were more like small shorts that covered almost everything, including the navel, rather than skimpy triangles of cloth that covered very little. It wasn't until movies like *Where the Boys Are*, starring Connie Francis, and the beach party movies of Frankie Avalon

Hotel Markham swimming pool *Paul Jermyn collection.*

Lion head fountain at the Hotel Markham pool. *From Dan Ellis.*

A typical bathing
suit of the day.

and Annette Funicello that the bikini became popular. Brian Hyland's
1960 hit record "Itsy, Bitsy, Teenie, Weenie, Yellow Polka Dot Bikini"
highlighted how the small bathing suits were not yet commonly seen on
the beaches.

For accessories, girls kept the real sparkle for dances and would even wear
their mothers' earrings to enhance their eveningwear. During the day, they
were more casual but still liked wearing some jewelry. Pins, signet rings and
class rings, ID bracelets and charm bracelets were very popular additions.
Charm bracelets were particularly popular, since the charms made perfect

gifts from families and boyfriends. Charms could be chosen for special occasions like a heart for Valentine's Day.

During the mid-'50s, pointed-toe shoes with spiked heels for women became almost universal for dressy occasions. The shoes were not very practical for walking, but the precarious nature was part of their appeal. They made women feel glamorous and free. The shoes were noticeably longer because of the pointed toes. The desire for a sharp profile was apparently more important than comfort.

For casual wear, the spikes were definitely not practical, so a lower, thick-heeled pump was the choice. Shoes called baby dolls were worn around the house or for just hanging out. They got their name from their round toes resembling a doll's shoes. While the casual pumps were mostly in black, the baby dolls came in many fun colors.

Sandals were also big in Gulfport in the '50s. Most casual sandals had low, chunky heels. To avoid embarrassing accidents, an ankle strap called a sling back was wrapped around the heel to keep the foot from slipping out. These sling backs were featured on other styles as well, such as pumps and wedges.

Every girl wore flats. Most featured heels that were less than half an inch, but the really trendy shoes were totally flat with no heels at all. In the brand-conscious '50s, flats by Capezio were the choice of most girls who could afford them. These pricey shoes had sharp toes, no heels, low sides and were cut deeply enough in front to expose toe cleavage. Capezio and Bernardo, two famous brands, produced a lace-up flat called ghillies. These shoes featured long straps that were wrapped around the calf, similar to the long straps on espadrilles. Girls tried various new ways to tie the straps but found that tying them in the back of the ankle worked best.

Stockings were a must for women, and only during the extreme Gulfport heat would women go out without them. At that time, girls wouldn't think of even wearing sandals without stockings.

Saddle oxford shoes were worn by teenage boys and girls, as well as their mothers. Saddle oxfords were made of one color, usually white or tan, with clay pot–colored rubber soles. A contrasting leather "saddle" across the middle of these lace-up shoes gave them the name. Gulfport teenagers also wore white bucks or nubucks. These shoes were like saddle oxfords without the contrasting leather across the instep. The white color made the bucks easy to scuff. To maintain their clean appearance, a small bag of chalk powder or a stick of chalk was carried to use at the sight of the first mark. The members of the Gulfport High School marching band wore white bucks as part of their uniform.

Although there had been a period in Gulfport in which strapless shoes were the "thing," their popularity had diminished. But toward the end of the '50s, there was a surge in popularity of T-strap shoes, which led to a return of the traditional straps. Shoes as diverse as evening shoes and sandals were now designed with straps. Some girls wore Mary Jane shoes, which were oxford shoes or flats with a single strap across the instep. Mary Janes were named after the sweetheart of Buster Brown in the *Buster Brown* comic strip, who wore similar shoes.

Loafers and moccasins were the most practical casual shoe. They were easy to slip on and could be worn with bobby socks or no socks at all. Although loafers had been around since the 1930s, it wasn't until Bass started making its own brand of loafers called Weejuns that they became so popular. Weejuns had a strap across the top of the shoe simply for style. This strap featured a split design that was supposed to look like a pair of lips. People started placing shiny new pennies in the strap to add a little sparkle, and although the use of pennies was originally associated with Bass Weejuns, it became synonymous with an entire '50s fashion known as the penny loafer.

In Gulfport, there was a wide variety of hairstyles for teenage girls from pageboy, bouffant and headband to butch cuts and pixies. Toward the end of the '50s, the short and shaggy look was a favored style made popular by Italian movie stars like Gina Lollobrigida and Sophia Loren, and such American actors as Suzanne Pleshette. In the early to mid-'50s, almost all young Gulfport girls kept boxes of bobby pins on their dressers to secure pin curls. Short hair parted on the side with curls over and in front of the ear was a favored style. But the style that became a '50s trademark was the ponytail, the perfect accessory to the poodle skirt, bobby socks and saddle shoes.

By the late '50s, plastic rollers had replaced bobby pins and metal clips as pin curls became outdated. Many girls endured a nighttime of agony sleeping on rollers so their plumped-up hair would have bounce and fullness for the next day. In the early '60s, the beehive took over as the universal style—the higher the better. Teasing became a new art, and cans of hair spray became a necessity.

Chapter 5

FROM RADIO TO TELEVISION AND BACK

*S*pooky organ music swelled in the background as the familiar sound of a squeaking door announced the start of one of the nation's favorite radio programs. An eerie voice greeted the listeners with, "Good evening, friends of the Inner Sanctum. This is your host. I'm glad you came tonight, because we have a very special guest of horror with us. I'd like you to meet the late Johnny Gravestone. If you're looking for a job," the host would chuckle, "there's a good opening in the graveyard—not much pay, but with tomb and board. Ha-ha-ha-ha!" It was quite obvious from his cemetery humor that the program was more tongue-in-cheek than fright.

The year was 1950, and like so many other radio listeners across the country, people in Gulfport were tuned to the popular radio melodrama *Inner Sanctum*. The stories on the show were heavy with haunted mansions, supernatural spooks and other cliché horror characters that were never really meant to be what they seemed. The show was a farce that ended with a humorous twist to the otherwise chilling tales. We all accepted that the stories were spoofs. That was part of the appeal, and we enjoyed playing along.

In the 1940s and early 1950s, radios were the primary source of entertainment in our homes. Before the growing popularity of television in the mid-'50s, the entire family would gather around the receiver to listen to their favorite shows, many of which were broadcast live. Because of the vacuum tubes, capacitors, coils and other necessary components, most of the radios were large floor models. The cabinets were beautiful pieces of furniture that were relatively expensive. Some of the more popular brands were Zenith, Magnavox and Philco. Although FM had not yet been introduced, almost all of the old radios had shortwave bands that allowed us to tune in to police frequencies as well as stations all over the world.

This new form of entertainment gave us programs that kept us transfixed. Radio could paint captivating images in our minds of thrilling adventures, mysteries and romance in a way that real pictures could never do. Soap operas, quiz shows, comedies and children's shows were very popular on radio, just as they would later become on television. Music, of course, was a big part of the programming that was featured on variety hours, talent shows and such megahits as *The Grand Ole Opry*. For the first time, we could listen to play-by-play sports as if we were actually at a game; at times, the announcers would even enhance what was really happening on the field. We got the latest news in real time, and we tuned in to get the latest weather and fishing reports.

Our parents listened to classical music on programs like *The Voice of Firestone* and *The New York Philharmonic*. One of the more popular shows was the *Lux Radio Theater*, named after its sponsor, Lux Soap. The programs were adaptations of popular movies and Broadway plays, which exposed the audience to many great works that they would not have otherwise known.

Other radio shows that Gulfport families enjoyed together were sitcoms like *Amos 'n' Andy*, *Burns and Allen*, *Meet Corliss Archer*, *Our Miss Brooks*, *Lum and Abner* and *The Adventures of Ozzie and Harriet*. Westerns and adventure shows like *The Cisco Kid*, *The Lone Ranger*, *Hopalong Cassidy*, *Superman* and *Captain Midnight* were hits. In addition to *Inner Sanctum*, there were other popular mystery shows. *The Shadow* was one of the highest rated.

The introduction to *The Shadow* was as iconic as the introduction to *Inner Sanctum*. The show would open with its theme song, sinister organ music from a portion of the classical piece "Le Touet d'Omphale" by Camille Saint-Saëns, as the mysterious voice of the Shadow (played by Orson Welles) would say, "Who knows what evil lurks in the hearts of men? The Shadow knows!" Each program would end with the Shadow's warning: "The weed of crime bears bitter fruit. Crime does not pay…The Shadow knows!"

The Shadow, whose real name was Lamont Cranston, had learned an ancient technique while in the Orient that allowed him to "cloud men's minds" so they could not see him. This did not mean that he could literally become invisible but was an interesting shtick that allowed Cranston to interact with criminals without being detected.

Saturday morning radio shows were as popular with children in Gulfport as the Saturday morning television shows are with children today. One of our favorite programs came on at 8:00 a.m. every Saturday morning, featuring Big Jon as the host along with his friend Sparkie, a little elf from the land of make-believe. Sparkie would open with, "Hi, hey, hello kids, hi boys and girls, hi kids, come in here right now because it's time for Big Jon and Spark-i-e-e-e!" Then came the familiar theme song, "The Teddy Bears' Picnic." "If you go down in the woods today, you're sure of a big surprise… today's the day the teddy bears have their picnic." Sparkie was actually the voice of Jon "Big Jon" Arthur, speeded up in the same way that years later David Seville would become the voice of the Chipmunks. Sparkie's greatest wish was to one day become a real boy.

Everyone looked forward to the exciting escapades of Captain Jupiter and the fun characters that were a part of each episode. Jupiter was always fighting two villains, Montmorency Clutchrider and Ivan Crusingspeed, although we only knew these two villains by their names; they were never actually included in the action on any of the shows.

As a regular feature, Big Jon would sing "Happy Birthday" to kids in the listening audience. He never used the traditional birthday song but had a couple different ones of his own. One of my favorites was "Today is a birthday I wonder for whom, I know it's for someone who's right in this room. So, look all around you for somebody who…is smiling and happy… my goodness it's you. We congratulate you and pray good luck follows too, so Happy Birthday [name] from all of us to you."

The show was so convincing that we were all sure that Sparkie was real. Children wanted more than anything to see exactly what this little elf looked like. Finally, one day, Big Jon made a special offer. If we would send in our name and address, we would receive an autographed picture of Sparkie. Wow! That blew my mind. I was going to see my little friend at last. After waiting for what turned out to be a couple months, the envelope finally arrived in the mail. My hands were trembling with excitement as I tore into the package, expecting to see a photo of an actual elf. I was shocked and disappointed to find only a postcard with nothing more than a cheaply drawn cartoon character in some sort of space suit. What a disappointment. The program was never the same. The fantasy about Sparkie the little elf from the land of make-believe had been shattered. This made me and my friends realize that our imaginations were the magical power of radio. It would have been better to keep Sparkie in our minds rather than to see him on paper.

Let's Pretend was another of my favorite Saturday morning programs. This award-winning show featured adaptations of classic fairy tales like "Hansel and Gretel" and "Cinderella," as well as original stories like "The Youth Who Learned to Shiver and Shake" and "The Enchanted Frog." The programs were always inspirational, promoting the virtues of honesty and responsibility.

The thing I remember most about the show was its sponsor, Cream of Wheat. The show would begin with the sponsor's popular theme song: "Cream of Wheat is so good to eat and we have it every day. We sing this song and it makes us strong and it makes us shout hooray! It's good for growing babies and grownups, too, to eat. So, for all the family's breakfast, you can't beat Cream of Wheat." The announcer would then say, "The all American family cereal presents…*Let's Pretend.*" The host, Uncle Bill Adams, would greet everyone before the program began with, "Hello pretenders." Sitting on the floor in front of our big radio, my imagination took over as I hung on every word, following the adventure as if I were part of the story.

Gulfport had its own version of *Let's Pretend*. Once a week, Mrs. Ethelynd Baxley, the drama and speech teacher at Gulfport High School, produced a program on WGCM radio. The casts were made up of her drama students, and the subjects of the shows were also dramatizations of popular fairy tales and children's stories. One story was that of Robin Hood. Mrs. Baxley's students and *Let's Pretend* presented a version of the same tale. Many preferred Mrs. Baxley's interpretation to that of the national show.

Since many of our mothers were full-time homemakers, they would often have their radios tuned to their favorite daytime programs. Among the regular shows was *Don McNeill's Breakfast Club*. Like television talk shows today, the program had informal conversations with guest comedians, actors and singers, as well as members of the audience. McNeill also had a regular fifteen-minute segment he termed "Call to Breakfast." At that time, he would stop the activities for a march around the breakfast table. The audience seemed to enjoy it, and it made the listeners at home feel like they were an interactive part of the program.

Arthur Godfrey Time was another popular morning show in Gulfport. In addition to Arthur's comments and opinions about various topics, his show also included interviews with celebrities and performances by musical guests, along with his own musical group. He would often pick up his ukulele and plink out a tune. He is probably best remembered for having fired Julius LaRosa while on the air, a somewhat shocking incident at the time. LaRosa was a featured singer on the show who was just beginning to find success in the recording industry. His career was virtually destroyed after this confrontation.

Chesterfield Cigarettes was one of Arthur Godfrey's longest sponsors. A longtime smoker himself, Godfrey would suggest, "Buy 'em by the carton." Sorry to say, he developed lung cancer in his later years and eventually died from the disease.

In addition to the talk shows, soap operas were probably the most listened to programs on radio. One of Gulfport's favorites was *Oxydol's Own Ma Perkins*. As was often the case, the shows became associated with their sponsors. The setting of the show was a small town called Rushville Center, with Ma as the main character. Interestingly, Ma owned a lumberyard— not a profession one would expect a woman to have, particularly in the '50s. Shuffle Shober was her best friend, with whom she shared her trials and tribulations. Ma Perkins was a kind-hearted woman who offered wise advice to her friends and neighbors who always seem to find themselves in some dilemma.

Our Gal Sunday, on the other hand, was more like what one expects a soap opera to be. Sunday was an orphan living in Colorado. She grew up to marry a wealthy British aristocrat, Arthur Brinthrope, who owned a silver mine in the small town. Her mother had abandoned Sunday and left her on the doorsteps of a crusty mining couple named Jackie and Lively. She was given the name "Sunday" for the day of the week on which she was discovered. The show always opened with a question that encapsulated the whole story line: "Can this girl from the little mining town in the West find happiness as the wife of a wealthy and titled Englishman?" "Red River Valley," the theme song of the show, played in the background.

For a true dose of melodrama, *The Romance of Helen Trent* topped my mother's list. The program would open with the announcer explaining the premise of the show: "And now, *The Romance of Helen Trent*, the real-life drama of Helen Trent, who, when life mocks her, breaks her hopes, dashes her against the rocks of despair, fights back bravely, successfully, to prove what so many women long to prove, that because a woman is 35 or more, romance in life need not be over, that romance can begin at 35." Helen Trent was always 35 even though the show ran for many years.

Throughout the 1950s, radio shows continued to be a regular source of entertainment for Gulfport families. However, with the growing popularity of television in the mid-'50s, the number of these programs began to decline. Although television had been created in the late 1920s, it didn't grow into a serious medium, mainly because of a freeze in development prompted by World War II. The restrictions were lifted after the war, but sales remained slow. The numbers were low because there were few sets available, and the high cost of a set was prohibitive for many. Only a small number of people owned a television before 1947, but as the cost of the sets became more reasonable, the numbers jumped dramatically so that by 1955, at least half of the homes in America had their own TV.

Most of us had watched our first real television while standing on the sidewalk in downtown Gulfport in front of the Western Auto's store on 25th Avenue. Management had placed two or three sets in the large front window and would leave the televisions on after the store closed. Since it was common in those days to have people downtown shopping late into the evening, there was always a small group of curiosity seekers glued to the Western Auto window, many of whom were seeing television for the first time.

As was common in early television, at least one of these sets seemed to always need adjustment. The weak signal coming from New Orleans or Mobile would often result in problems. A "horizontal hold" control knob on the sets would usually correct one of the most irritating glitches. The picture would appear to be rolling over from bottom to top. There was no one at the store after hours to adjust the sets, so the window shoppers had to overlook these minor glitches. The people were excited just to see anything on television, even if the picture was so "snowy" at times they could barely make out the images.

Television had a positive effect on many of us by bringing families together. Children and parents gathered to enjoy such family-oriented shows as *I Love Lucy* and *The Adventures of Ozzie and Harriet*. It was easy to shift to the new medium, as some of the radio shows we enjoyed moved to television. The formats of the early programs were mostly modeled after the radio shows.

Many were only fifteen minutes long, including news broadcasts like the pioneering *Camel News Caravan*, hosted by John Cameron Swayze. Swayze was a newspaper journalist before moving to television in 1949. He became one of the first popular television personalities. The show, sponsored by Camel Cigarettes, incorporated interviews and commentaries along with actual live shots of news events, something unheard of before television. Swayze would open the newscast with, "Hopscotching the world for headlines," a lead-in that became identified with him and the program.

His most famous line, however, was associated with his longtime sponsor. When he said, "It takes a licking and keeps on ticking," we all knew he meant a Timex watch.

As television grew, the format began to change and move away from radio-style programming. This led to such innovative shows as NBC's *Today*, which debuted in 1952, and various sitcoms with memorable and enduring characters, like Wally and the Beaver on *Leave It to Beaver*, Barney Fife on *The Andy Griffith Show* and Wally Cox as *Mr. Peepers*. As with radio, several children's shows were produced. ABC's *The Mickey Mouse Club* was enormously popular, particularly with young boys, who often tuned in just to see the maturing Annette Funicello, the most popular Mouseketeer.

WDSU-TV Channel 6 in New Orleans was the most watched station in Gulfport and along the coast because it had the strongest signal. It started broadcasting in 1948 and was not only the first television station in Louisiana but was also one of the first fifty stations in the United States. We could also receive WALA-TV Channel 10 in Mobile, but the signal was not quite as strong. Since both stations were NBC affiliates, we were more inclined to watch New Orleans. Television brought us closer to the city of New Orleans than we had ever been before, keeping us informed about the news, weather and happenings around town.

Local programs were common on early television. These homegrown shows helped launch the careers of several national personalities. Dick Van Dyke was one of the more successful entertainers who started on WDSU-TV. Since Gulfport was too small to have its own television stations at that time, we all watched the New Orleans stations as if they were our own.

There were several popular local children's shows over the years, beginning with the *Captain Sam Show*, one of the earliest children's shows in the South. Captain Sam featured children in a peanut gallery similar to the later *Howdy Doody Show*. There was also Mrs. Muffin on *Mrs. Muffin's Birthday Party* and *The Great McNutt*, host of the afternoon *Three Stooges* shorts. McNutt was a colorful character who dressed in the iconic movie director's outfit, complete with jodhpurs and a large megaphone. He started each movie yelling through his megaphone, "Lights, camera, action, start the cotton pickin' show!"

The Midday Show was an hour-long show on WDSU featuring local news, entertainment, music and conversation hosted by Steve Summers, Iris Kelso, Terry Flettrich and Al Shea. Flettrich is most remembered for her years and many roles at WDSU. She joined WDSU before the station started on the

Terry Flettrich.

air. Over her many years at the station, she served as a writer, producer and on-air personality, and early on was Mrs. Muffin on the children's show.

Another popular co-host of *Midday* was Wayne Mack, although he is most familiar to youngsters as "the Great McNutt." Wayne was also a distinguished sportscaster on the station, along with Hap Glaudi and Buddy Diliberto.

Second Cup was a morning show starring Bob and Jan Carr. The husband-and-wife team featured topics of interest to young families. Jan, who had been a Rockette at Radio City Music Hall in New York before coming to New Orleans, was up to date on fashion. She highlighted the latest trends as a feature of their program. *Second Cup* was broadcast from the top of the Royal Orleans Hotel in a casual setting. After their show ended, Bob and Jan joined *Midday*.

There have been several notable newsmen on WDSU. Alec Gifford was with the station for years not only as the news anchor at noon on *Midday* but also on the evening news as the "Esso Reporter."

Tiger Flowers was one of the more recognizable reporters at the station, not only for his long run at WDSU but also for his quirky name. The laid-back ease with which he reported news events and sports was hardly ferocious like his name would imply.

Bill Monroe was probably the most successful newsman to ever have worked at the station. Monroe began his work at WDSU as an editorial writer whose editorials were delivered on air not only by himself but also by Mel Leavitt and Jerry Romig. He later left New Orleans to become the station's Washington, D.C. bureau chief. He was subsequently selected to be the moderator of NBC's *Meet the Press*.

Mel Leavitt was best known as a sportscaster who was teamed with Nash Roberts, the weatherman. They appeared together after the evening news. Leavitt was also seen on a program that followed NBC's *Tonight Show* called *Tonight with Mel*. The show had a similar format to the *Tonight Show*. Mel interviewed celebrity guests, local VIPs and various entertainers. He was also seen on *Byline*, an afternoon show that introduced us to celebrities who were visiting the city. Mel Leavitt was so popular as a regular on WDSU that he became known as "Mr. Television" in New Orleans.

Nash Roberts was the first full-time meteorologist in the South. He was one of the original employees of WDSU-TV when the station first started. His weather forecasts were seen during the 5:00 p.m., 6:00 p.m. and 10:00 p.m. newscasts. He also reported the weather on the *Midday* program. Nash's brother Ep Roberts, who was also a meteorologist, would fill in for Nash

Mel Leavitt.

when he was not available. Ep also had his own spot on the morning show *Breakfast Edition* on WDSU. Nash would show us his weather forecast by drawing with a black marker on a large map of the United States covered in clear plastic. It is a far cry from the radar maps used by meteorologists on television today.

Scoop Kennedy was a newsman who traded his career in news for his real love for cooking. He changed his name to "Chef" Kennedy as the host of his own cooking show on WDSU. He soon became recognized as one of the great chefs of New Orleans. Marie Mathews, another excellent cook, assisted him on the show.

One of the most memorable and endearing characters on New Orleans television was not a real person at all but rather a puppet that we only saw a few weeks a year. Mr. Bingle was a creation of the marketing department of Maison Blanche department store as a mascot to promote the store during the Christmas season. This snuggly white snowman with a red pointed hat was introduced as an assistant to Santa Claus. Mr. Bingle had the same initials as Maison Blanche, which was often referred to as "MB." The little

Nash Roberts.

snowman was an immediate success, appearing in radio and television commercials and greeting children in puppet shows throughout the city. His continuing success through the years can also be attributed to his famous jingle. Everyone in New Orleans, in Gulfport and along the coast can probably still sing the Mr. Bingle theme song:

> *Jingle, jangle, jingle*
> *Here comes Mr. Bingle*
> *With another message from Kris Kringle*
> *Time to launch your Christmas season*
> *Maison Blanche makes Christmas pleasin'*
> *Gifts galore for you to see*
> *Each a gem from MB!*

In 1957, Screen Gems released a collection of old Universal Studios horror movies for syndication. Universal suggested that a host be used to introduce the films. This led to the creation of "horror hosts" throughout the country. Vampira (Maila Nurmi) was the first television horror show host. She set the format, tone and mood of the other horror hosts and shows that followed, including Elvira (Cassandra Peterson) in the '80s and '90s. *The Vampira Show* actually premiered in 1954, three years before Screen Gems released the movie package, making her a true original. Vampira's tongue-in-cheek horror comments amused the viewers. She would poke fun at the movie that was on that night and would talk to her pet spider, Rollo. Among other quirky things, she called for her fans to send in requests for epitaphs rather than autographs.

On Saturday night, January 3, 1959, at 10:30 p.m., WWL-TV introduced one of the most unique and successful stars to emerge in New Orleans television. Although now in his nineties and long retired, Morgus the Magnificent, the late-night host of *House of Shock*, continues to be a favorite in New Orleans and along the coast after all these years.

Morgus the Magnificent became so popular that his show continued in various forms into the 1980s. New Orleans actor Sid Noel portrayed Momus Alexander Morgus, or Doctor Morgus, a mad scientist who conducted experiments throughout the show that coincided with the theme of that night's movie. Chopsley, his assistant, was an executioner and never spoke a word on the program. Chopley's face was never shown because he wore an executioner's hood. According to the story, Chopsley was a former classmate of Morgus's in medical school. In typical fashion, the wacky experiments

Vampira.

that Morgus and Chopsley conducted with good intentions sometimes failed or blew up in their faces.

The name of the show derived from the label on the package from Universal Studio marked "Shock." The name led to many of the early programs being called "Shock Theater" or some variation of that title. The

Morgus the Magnificent.

whole concept was so successful that a second package of films was released in 1958 called *Son of Shock*.

Although radio was no longer the force it had once been, radio was not dead. The widespread use of the new transistors ultimately saved radio as a viable source of entertainment. The first transistor radio went on sale in 1954. It was slightly larger than a pack of cigarettes and cost $49.95 at Western Auto, among other places in Gulfport. The new transistors allowed radios to be much smaller and more durable and use less electricity.

To power the new radios, a special nine-volt battery was developed. These nine-volt batteries have now become a common power source for many other electrical devices we use today. After the transistor radio's initial success, Sony continued to make the radios even smaller and more efficient, until by 1962 they sold for as little as fifteen dollars.

We never stopped loving radio; we just loved it in a different way. With the popularity of the transistor, radio became our companion, as we were conveniently able to take our music with us wherever we went.

Chapter 6

OUR LOCAL BANDS AND TOP 40 RADIO

*L*ate one evening in 1954, I was in my room surfing the airwaves on my Philco radio before retiring for the night. The lights were low, and my parents had long been asleep. Since many of the lower-wattage AM stations cut their power in the evening to avoid interfering with other stations, my choice of stations was limited. I eventually tuned to our familiar WWL 870 AM out of New Orleans, one of the nation's few fifty-thousand-watt clear channel stations. These powerful stations could be heard over five hundred miles away at night without interference.

That evening, the music was being broadcast live from the Blue Room of the Roosevelt Hotel. The Blue Room had gained a reputation as one of the country's top entertainment sites, featuring musicians like Louis Armstrong, Jan Garber and a local favorite, Leon Kelner on piano. Kelner also had his own TV show in the '50s in New Orleans.

But that night, I was bored with the smooth sounds coming from the Blue Room, so I started running through the stations from the top of the dial to the bottom, hoping to find something more stimulating. As I slowly turned the amber-lighted channel selector, stations faded in and out. Occasionally, I would hear a garbled Spanish voice in the distant background as the radio frequencies overlapped.

On the far end of the dial, I stopped short. As I locked into a station at 1510 AM, I could not believe what I was hearing. It was the sound of a guitar moaning as if it were in pain, while a black man sang from deep in his soul, "The sky is crying, look at the tears roll down the street…"

When the song ended, an announcer with a deep, gravelly voice came on: "Hey, everybody, John R. way down south in the middle of Dixie, I'm back on the scene and I'm back with Ernie's. You ready for that…" The station was clear channel WLAC in Nashville, Tennessee; the singer was Elmore James; the announcer was John R. (real name John Richbourg), and he was talking about Ernie's Record Mart. I was blown away. I continued listening, reveling in the newly discovered blues sounds I was hearing for the first time, songs by Lightnin' Hopkins, Muddy Waters, Little Junior Parker, the Spaniels, Sonny Boy Williamson, Etta James and Howling Wolf. I was hooked.

I had stumbled onto something special. I later learned that John R. had taken over the show from Gene Nobles, another one of the four deejays who made up the nightly rotation on WLAC. The four came to be known as the "fifty-thousand-watt quartet." The listeners were at first surprised to discover the deejays were not black men at all but actually

John R. (Richbourg). *From Jim Lowe.*

middle-aged white guys who sounded black. They not only sounded black but also developed a "black persona" using street talk and expressions to appeal to their black listeners.

The first and most famous of the four was Gene Nobles, whose sponsor was Randy's Record Shop in Gallatin, Tennessee. "Randy" was Randy Wood, a record store owner who had originally opened his shop to sell appliances. He began carrying a few records in the back of the store and soon realized that white kids in sizable numbers were beginning to ask for records by black artists such as Wynonie Harris, Ivory Joe Hunter and the Ravens. Sensing a growing market, he increased his stock. The record sales became so successful that he eventually phased out the appliances and changed the store to Randy's Record Shop. He and Nobles experimented with selling some of his records on the air. The program became very popular with black people and also began gradually appealing to young whites who were just beginning to discover the blues. As a result of the show on WLAC, Randy's Record Shop grew into what was advertised as the "World's Largest Mail-Order Phonograph

Randy's Record Shop. *From Jim Lowe.*

Record Shop," and because of the strength of the radio station, Gene Nobles's program was probably the most listened to radio show at night at that time all over the country.

Gene Nobles became the first white man to play popular black music regularly on the radio, long before deejays like Alan Freed, Dick Biondi, Clark Weber, Cousin Brucie and Wolfman Jack made the scene. Before Nobles's late-night show, black R&B artists were mostly heard at live performances in juke joints on the so-called Chitlin' Circuit. At that time, black records were only purchased by black poeple in black-owned record stores and were almost never heard on the radio except on low-wattage stations on the fringe areas around larger radio markets like New York and Chicago. The signals on these smaller stations were weak, and the shows hardly cleared the boundaries of the black neighborhoods.

Gene Nobles was known for his use of double entendré. Once, he was disciplined for making suggestive comments about the use of one of the show's regular sponsors, Royal Crown Petroleum Jelly. Nobles was also known for using made-up words and phrases that he called "slanguage." He would spell out words using jumbled up syllables: "OK everybody," he would say, "the Wednesday night dance hour is on the air brought to you by…Reazoil [Royal] Creazound [Crown] the he is there [Hair] the dree is epic [Dressing] Royal Crown Hair Dressing and Royal Crown Pomade, the light bright modern way to keep your hair looking smooth." He referred to boys as "jerks" and girls as "fillies." One of his more common expressions was, "from the heart of my bottom," a suggestive twist on the well-known phrase.

One of the popular commercials on Gene's show featured Little Richard. Richard would say, "Slippin' and slidin' Gene Nobles with that good word on Royal Crown Hair Dressing. Everywhere I go, and I go just about everywhere, the girls are really gone on Royal Crown Hair Dressing. Even old Long Tall Sally uses it. You know something, Gene, I go for the girl with the Royal Crown look, 'cause, man, um…she's got it."

With the success of his record store, Randy Wood formed his own recording company, Dot Records. He wanted to cash in on the growing popularity of R&B music by introducing it to white audiences. But to do that, he had to have white singers cover the black songs. His first artist, a young twenty-year-old Charles Eugene "Pat" Boone, had his first number-one hit as a cover of the Fats Domino song "Ain't That a Shame." After that song topped the charts, Pat Boone covered other Fats Domino songs, which far outsold the originals. Fats later acknowledged to Dick Clark that without Pat Boone, the world would have never discovered Fats Domino.

Using the same successful formula, Randy Wood had Boone cover songs by other black artists like Little Richard's "Tutti Frutti" and "Long Tall Sally." Other white artists on Wood's Dot label also had hits with cover songs. Gale Storm topped the charts with "I Hear You Knocking," originally a record by Smiley Lewis, and the Fontane Sisters did the same with "Hearts of Stone" by the Jewels, also a popular release for Otis Williams and the Charms.

When Gene Nobles's health forced him to leave the air temporarily, WLAC filled his spot with newsman John Richbourg. Richbourg continued Nobles's practice of playing R&B and blues records, which he called "cornfield." His playing of "race records" received a lot of criticism from white conservatives, although overall he was very popular with the listeners. After so many fans misspelled his name when writing to him at the station, John Richbourg began calling himself John R. to make it simpler.

When John R. made the permanent switch from newsman to deejay, he became the regular host of another mail-order record business, Ernie's Record Mart. Ernie Young founded Nashbro records as well as a record distributing company in Nashville. He opened Ernie's Record Mart to sell the 45s that he took off the jukeboxes he serviced. Ernie's gave Randy's stiff competition. The show was heard every night beginning at 10:00 p.m. and opened with the rocking beat of "Swannee River Boogie" by Albert Ammons. As the theme song began, a voice would call out, "Hey, John R. watcha gonna do…Come on John R. and play me some rhythm and blues…"

John R. and his R&B records began attracting young white teenagers who were interested not only in the music they had never heard before but also his "street talk." Those of us who had discovered WLAC tuned in discreetly, almost as if we were members of an underground society listening to something we were not supposed to hear. We would close ourselves in our rooms, grooving in the wee hours to the blues—music that would not have been understood by our parents or many of our "square" friends at school.

Following John R. came a show called *After Hours*. The name came from the title of the opening theme song by Avery Parish. Hosted by Herman Grizzard, the show ran from midnight to 3:00 a.m. Like the other WLAC personalities, Grizzard was also sponsored by a popular mail-order record store, Buckley's Record Shop. Located near the Vanderbilt University campus on Church Street in Nashville, Buckley's carried mostly local artists, whom Grizzard would feature on his program.

Bill "Hoss" Allen (The Hossman) took over Gene Nobles's time slot when Gene retired permanently. Hoss specialized in gospel groups like the Dixie Hummingbirds, the Golden Gate Quartet and Sister Rosetta Tharpe. All three sponsors—Randy's Record Shop, Ernie's Record Mart and Buckley's Record Shop—provided a way for teenagers to get music that was otherwise not available in their regular stores, or at least not at ones that many of us would frequent.

On each program, the record store sponsors would offer select groups of 45 rpm records, usually five in a package, that were given identifying names like "Ernie's Bullseye Special" or "Randy's Soul Review." The deejays would play some of the records from each package to highlight the selections. The groups were sold at a discount price, although the five would usually include one or two throw-in records that none of us would probably have purchased otherwise. Richbourg was the perfect pitchman for Ernie's: "John R. here for Ernie's, the one and only Ernie's Record Mart. Man they got 'em... records galore at that store. Specializing in sending them out too, by mail, COD...unconditionally guaranteed."

When not selling records, Richbourg was also known for selling offbeat products like baby chicks from Wright's Poultry Farms. John R. would say, "Listen here, friends. Everybody likes fried chicken, right? How would you like to have fried chicken on your table? I've got an offer for you that will put that fried chicken on your table just about any time you want it, huh? Look here, baby, you can...you can if you just listen to old John R. I got an offer for you that will put that fried chicken on your table in no time. Wright's Poultry Farms will send you 110 of the finest baby chicks that you ever saw for the low, low price of just $2.95 plus 50 cents handling charge plus COD charge."

Authentic R&B and blues like the records featured on WLAC were not available at our local record store. Before Randy's and the other mail-order shops, we bought all of our records from Oberlies Record Store in Gulfport. In the 1950s, the music could only be heard live in the black clubs in Gulfport. Local and well-known blues and R&B acts played the joints in north Gulfport along a strip of old Highway 49, now called Arkansas Avenue. The clubs like the Hi-Hat, the Silver Moon, the Cotton Club, the Evangeline Club, the Beverly Lounge and Little Conway's were outside the Gulfport city limits and therefore out of the jurisdiction of the law.

Oberlies Record Shop. *Clayton Rand Papers, Manuscripts Division, Special Collections Department, Mississippi State University Libraries.*

Teenagers who were into the blues could hear some of the greatest artists of the time without having their IDs checked.

A popular entertainment site for the black community was the North Gulfport Auditorium, located across from the Shiloh Baptist Church on what is now Martin Luther King Jr. Boulevard. This dance hall presented such greats as James Brown, Ike and Tina Turner, Etta James, Professor Longhair, Sam Cooke and a host of others. These musicians would play there after performing at the 100 Men Hall in Bay St. Louis. The hall was part of the famous Chitlin' Circuit. After their shows, the entertainers would stay at a small hotel on the same street near the auditorium in Gulfport, one of the only hotels in the city that would accommodate black people during that period.

One of the most famous blues piano players who played the strip was Roosevelt Sykes. He lived in Gulfport during the '50s and wrote a tribute to the city, the clubs on 49 and Charles Conway's club, where he was the

Roosevelt Sykes.

headliner. "Gulfport Boogie" was a rollicking record about the city he loved most: "Jumpin' and jivin' til the break of day, you'll go rockin' at Little Conway's....I've been a long time on Highway 49."

Carl Gates, band director at the black high school on Gulfport's 33rd Avenue, produced some of the top musicians on the coast. Gates was also a promoter who brought big-name blues acts to Gulfport, artists like Willie Willis, Henry Townsend, Little Milton, Tyrone Davis, Slim Harpo and

Jimmy Reed.

Jimmy Reed. In 1955, there were only a few black artists who made the top 100 on the Billboard charts, although there were several of the cover records in the top 20. All of that was about to change.

One evening, I was sitting in the Paramount Theater in downtown Gulfport waiting for the movie to start. The movie was *The Blackboard Jungle*, a film of teenage rebellion, starring Glenn Ford, Vic Morrow and a young Sidney Poitier. Bam! The movie opened with a blast, and the audience was slammed with the raw sounds of rock 'n' roll: "One, two, three o'clock, four o'clock rock…" The music scene would never be the same from then on.

"Rock Around the Clock," by Bill Haley and the Comets, not only was the first rock 'n' roll song ever used in a feature film, but it also introduced rock 'n' roll music to mainstream America.

When teenagers began to discover that Pat Boone's hit songs were actually covers of black artists, they began to seek out the originals. Fats Domino's "Blueberry Hill" hit the pop charts in 1956, marking the beginning of acceptance of songs by Little Richard, Chuck Berry and others, although many parents would still not allow their children to bring "race" records into the home. Several black artists made Billboard's top 100 in 1956. There were the Platters, Frankie Lymon and the Teenagers, Bill Doggett, the Five Satins, Howlin' Wolf, Shirley and Lee, LaVern Baker, Screamin' Jay Hawkins, Big Maybelle, Ivory Joe Hunter, Little Willie John and, of course, Nat King Cole, whose sound was considered "white" enough not to offend.

The music of the '50s sparked a revolution that is continuing even today. Before that spark was ignited, however, teenagers and young adults listened to a variety of styles. Swing, blues and country were all popular in the day, but it was the music of the big seventeen-piece bands whose theme songs practically defined our parents' musical era. Benny Goodman's "Sing,

Paramount Theater. *From the Shaw Design Group collection.*

Sing, Sing," Glenn Miller's "In the Mood," Tommy Dorsey's "I'm Getting Sentimental Over You" and Duke Ellington's "Take the 'A' Train" were as popular as any of the other hits of that period.

The bands depended on radio airplay and record sales for success, just as they do today. Live performances were equally important, and many of the bands played grueling one-night stands throughout the country in order to reach their fans. Artists like Frank Sinatra, Doris Day, Ella Fitzgerald and, of course, Bing Crosby, the most innovative and popular star in the world in the late '40s, were idolized by our parents' generation just like the rock 'n' roll stars of the '50s. The success of Bing Crosby not only on records and radio but also in a series of popular movies introduced the idea that singers were not just novelty acts but were indeed genuine artists. It was the various musical styles of 1940s that helped pave the way for rock 'n' roll.

From its beginning in the '20s and continuing to the present, *The Grand Ole Opry*, a weekly live show on WSM 650 AM, was and is one of the most popular country music programs on radio. But we listened to a show out of Shreveport, Louisiana, that had an even greater impact on country music. *The Louisiana Hayride*, heard on the fifty-thousand-watt KWKH-AM, was admittedly an almost direct knock-off of *The Grand Ole Opry*, but there were a couple key differences. Whereas the *Opry* only featured established stars that had hit records, the *Hayride* showcased new artists and innovative musical styles, something *The Grand Ole Opry* would not have even considered. In addition, the *Opry* banned the use of electric guitars, while the *Hayride* actually embraced the instrument that would transform traditional country, blues and rockabilly into a new musical blending called rock 'n' roll.

The *Louisiana Hayride* not only helped launch the careers of country legends like Hank Williams, but it also gave a young nineteen-year-old Elvis Presley a crucial break in his career. Elvis had flopped on his debut at *The Grand Ole Opry*, but in October 1954, he gave a historic performance on *The Louisiana Hayride*. His rendition of "That's Alright, Mama" and "Blue Moon of Kentucky" jump-started his career.

On June 26, 1955, Elvis made his first appearance on the Mississippi Gulf Coast at the Slavonian Lodge Auditorium on the corner of Myrtle and First Streets in Biloxi. The popular local band Johnny Elmer and the Rockets played the Slavonian regularly and was scheduled to play that evening. But according to Salvadore "Penue" Taranto, a member of the Rockets band, they were asked to forfeit their gig that night to let Elvis play in their place. Although Elvis had his first record, "That's Alright, Mama," on the jukebox at that time, he was hardly a star. It was not until the next year that his career really took off with his first number-one hit, "Heartbreak Hotel," on RCA.

After performing at the Slavonian Lodge, Elvis played the next two nights at the Officers' Club at Keesler Air Force Base. Before his superstardom, Elvis usually performed in skating rinks and school gymnasiums throughout the southern states, making several appearances along the coast at places like the Pink Pony in Gulf Hills resort near Ocean Springs. During his performance at Keesler, he met June Juanico, a local Biloxi girl. June had never heard of Elvis before, but the meeting eventually led to a two-year relationship.

When not performing, Elvis was in the clubs and other locations along the beach. I met Elvis during his visit in 1955. My friends and I were having a blast at the Biloxi-Gulfport Amusement Park on Highway 90. On that particular evening, a crowd had gathered in front of Poston's Carpet Golf next door, pushing and shoving toward a car that was slowly moving through the parking lot. We worked our way closer to see the young man inside. He turned and flashed a boyish grin, shook our hands and then waved goodbye as he drove away onto Highway 90. The enthusiastic crowd had just met Elvis Presley. No one played miniature golf that evening; we were too excited.

With the explosion of rock 'n' roll, the music scene began to slowly shift away from the crooners of the '40s to the young artists who were following in Elvis's footsteps. The music was everything the suburban 1950s were not. Our parents were appalled that we were thrusting and grinding, bumping and twisting to a new beat—a beat that many ministers condemned as the music of Satan. As a result, rock 'n' roll records were banned from some local radio stations. Throughout the country, many were even burned in large bonfires during protest demonstrations. There were no such protests in Gulfport, but none of that mattered. The teenage rebellion was larger than any before for several reasons. The new prosperity of the '50s provided discretionary money for the purchase of records and record players. We had our own money to spend, and spend we did. By the end of the decade, the music pointed out the growing differences between modern teenagers and adults.

One of our favorite shows was *Your Hit Parade*. This popular television show actually chronicled the transition from the parents' pop music to the children's rock 'n' roll. We had first heard the show on radio before transitioning to television. The original name was *Your Hit Parade, America's Taste in Popular Music*, a perfect description for the show that was the first to highlight on a weekly basis the songs that were trending throughout the country. The radio show opened without music but rather with just the voice of the announcer giving what is probably one of the most iconic commercials in radio history. The announcer would say, "With men who know tobacco best, it's Luckies, two to one." Following that statement, we were all captivated by the sound of a tobacco auctioneer calling out prices in a hypnotic rhythm and ending in the words, "Sold to A-mer…i-can!" A tickertape or telegraph key began clicking as if a stock alert was coming over the wire, and then the announcer would say, "L-S…M-F-T... L-S…M-F-T," in the same pulsating rhythm. Another voice would add, "You said it! Lucky Strike means fine tobacco! So Round, so firm, so fully packed.…So free and easy on the draw!" The sound of the same auctioneer calling out numbers that none of us could ever understand was repeated, again ending with, "Sold to A-mer…i-can! Then the band would slide into the theme song, "This Is My Lucky Day," a song made popular in 1956 by Judy Garland. After the auctioneer did his thing twice, the announcer, André Baruch, would say, "Lucky Strike presents *Your Hit Parade* starring Kay Thompson, Charles Carlyle, Gogo De Lys and Johnny Hauser," names that were the original cast but changed over the years as new members replaced the old.

Your Hit Parade premiered on NBC television in 1950 and was an immediate success. The show was the first to count down the top seven songs of the week according to a music survey. We all waited in anticipation as the hits were counted down until finally the number-one song was revealed. But instead of the original artists performing their songs on the show, the songs were performed by one of the four regular cast vocalists. During the transition years to rock 'n' roll, Dorothy Collins, Russell Arms, Snooky Lanson and Gisèle MacKenzie were the featured singers, appearing in elaborate productions with thematic sets. The format worked great at first. The biggest problem the show faced was how to present new and different productions of the same song each week, since many landed on the chart for several weeks. But with the advent of Elvis Presley in the top spots, it became absurd to watch big-band singer Snooky Lanson's attempt to sing "Hound Dog" in different ridiculous settings week after week. Eventually, the television show died as the real artists and their performances became more important than the songs themselves. We wanted to see the actual performer, not some watered-down attempt to perform the rock 'n' roll hits by singers who had no feel for the new music at all.

When rock 'n' roll exploded on the scene in the mid-'50s, it profoundly affected the style of radio programming. A whole new relationship developed between the disk jockey, the music and the teenage audience. The crucial link was the deejay, who not only counted down the top records each week but also hosted record hops and Saturday night dances. Teens turned them into heroes, forming fan clubs and sending them personal photos and even home-baked cookies. These deejays often developed wild and zany personalities, sometimes becoming bigger than the stars they promoted. Radio stations realized the newfound marketing potential and began launching fun promotions and contests for girls to win a date with their favorite deejay.

As the stations throughout the country switched to a top 40 format, the lineup of big-name deejays swelled. New York had personalities like Alan Freed, Murray "The K" Kaufman, Jocko Henderson, Don Imus and others; Chicago had Dick Biondi and Howard Miller; Boston had Arnie "Woo-Woo" Ginsberg; Cleveland had Bill Randle; St. Louis had Jack Carney; Detroit had Robin Seymour; and San Francisco had Tom Donahue. In New Orleans, we listened to Dan Diamond, Jack "The Cat" Elliott, Jockey John Stone, Happy Herb Holiday, Bud Connell and the one deejay who was around the longest, Jim Stewart of WNOE.

The two rock 'n' roll stations that we listened to in Gulfport were New Orleans stations WNOE 1060 AM and WTIX 690 AM, referred to as "The mighty 690." Station owner Bob Storz was the first person to create the top 40 format that was soon universally adopted by most stations across the country. Because of Storz, WTIX was the first radio station in the country to have a top 40 show. Not to be outdone, the major competitor of WTIX, station WNOE, counted down the "Nifty Top Fifty."

Bob Storz was farsighted and saw the future of rock 'n' roll that merged black and white music, especially in New Orleans. Under his direction, WTIX became the first radio station in the nation to play the original black versions of the hits, along with white performers like Elvis, Jerry Lee Lewis and Buddy Holly.

The stations battled for the baby boomers, engaging in a spirited fight for the top spot. To get the audience's attention, they launched various contests, promotions and gimmicks. Reminiscent of Pavlov's dogs, WTIX introduced "chime time"; a chime was sounded when the time was given on the air. Those of us who listened to the two stations probably remember the WTIX

"Tenna Toppers." These orange Styrofoam balls were stuck on the tips of car radio antennas. Prizes were given to the listeners who spotted one of the balls when driving around town.

Before the structured top 40 formats, deejays were free to play records of their choice, and many played local musicians as well as national hits. This allowed for exposure to musical styles and artists that would never have normally been heard. A "Nifty Top 50" list from 1959 has some interesting entries. In addition to the top five ("I Want to Walk You Home" by Fats Domino, "What'd I Say" by Ray Charles, "Thank You, Pretty Baby" by Brook Benton, "There Goes My Baby" by the Drifters and "You're So Fine" by the Falcons), there were also records like "Cry" by the Nightsbridge Strings, "It's Too Late" by Tarheel Slim and Little Ann and "There Is Something on Your Mind" by Little Sonny. These were hardly well-known artists. Some deejays even cut their own records and played them on the air as well as at record hops and dances. Jockey John Stone of WNOE received airplay with his record "Mirror, Mirror," but it never got traction. One notable success was the "Green Door" by Jim Lowe, a deejay from WCBS in New York City. The record was released in 1956 on Dot Records and reached number one on the Billboard charts for the week of November 17, 1956. It bumped "Love Me Tender" by Elvis off the top spot.

WGCM 1240 AM in Gulfport was the oldest continuously broadcasting station on the coast and the second oldest in Mississippi. It began broadcasting upstairs in the M. Salloum building at the corner of 26th Avenue and 14th Street. In 1958, after moving to several different locations over the years, the station built a permanent studio and tower at the corner of 15th Avenue and 22nd Street. It never competed for the young crowd but rather continued playing the easy listening music of the '40s and '50s, although Tommy Meek, an announcer at the station, hosted a Saturday morning top 40 show called the *Hi-Fi Club* at the station's location on 22nd Street. It was broadcast live with teenagers in the studio.

WGCM was mostly known as the reliable source for news and information on the coast, broadcasting up-to-the-minute news reports, election returns, weather updates and other community services.

Several notable personalities broadcast on WGCM. House Democrat Whip Hale Boggs, father of Cokie Roberts of ABC News, worked as an announcer there while he studied law. Leonard Earl Campbell was another familiar announcer on WGCM. Campbell was a colorful character known as "The Gypsy." He began his career in the Ringling Brothers & Barnum and Bailey Circus as a clown. He left the circus and worked the vaudeville circuit, singing and playing piano. He performed at various locations on the coast for charity benefits as "Cleto" the clown. After World War II, he joined WGCM, hosting his own program called *The Voice of the Gypsy*. In 1948, the Gypsy created the I Am Your Neighbor Club to provide food for the needy. He would lead caravans to various people's homes to deliver much-needed food. His famous sign-off line on radio was, "If you're drinking, don't drive, and if you're driving, don't drink," a line inspired by the death of a five-

Leonard "The Gypsy" Campbell.

year-old boy he had witnessed, who was killed by a drunk driver. He was well loved by the common people of the city but was never accepted by the upper class in Gulfport. In fact, only one prominent businessman attended his funeral—a sad commentary about a man who did so much good for the people of the city.

Prior to the advent of top 40 radio and the rock 'n' roll bands that the new music spawned, there were several older musicians popular in Gulfport. Roosevelt Sykes was probably one of the more prominent, playing mostly at the clubs on Highway 49 in north Gulfport. He had been playing his form of piano-pounding boogie since 1921, when he first left home. He was only fifteen at the time, and while his style was rough at first, his music became more sophisticated as he matured, moving away from the traditional twelve-bar blues while adopting an eight-bar pop gospel style. He is given credit for writing "44 Blues," "Night Time Is the Right Time" and, of course, "Gulfport Boogie."

The Claudetts, a band from Pass Christian, were popular at some of our earlier dances. Isaac Joseph Darensbourg Jr., who became known as Guitar Bo, had been playing guitar around his hometown of Bay St.

The Claudetts. *From Bev Anderson.*

Louis with the Claudetts since he was a teenager. Jackie Avery played piano for a while with the group before moving on and writing several hits in both soul and country. Little Sonny Wimberly played bass with the Claudetts but left the group to join Muddy Waters's band in Chicago. After leaving the Claudetts, Guitar Bo signed on with M.C. Spencer & the Blue Flames, a band that we heard regularly at the Peppermint Lounge, a club in Biloxi on Veterans Avenue just a couple blocks from Gus Stevens. Spencer had discovered the vocalist Miss Dee while she was singing in a New Orleans bar. She joined Spencer's group and had already been singing with the Blue Flames before Guitar Bo came on board with the band.

When not playing music, Spencer was a schoolteacher in Biloxi. He finally gave up that job to concentrate on his music career. He moved his band to Oakland, California, to expand their opportunities. Although Miss Dee moved with the band, Guitar Bo chose to remain on the coast. Miss Dee and Guitar Bo had become close, and she tried to convince him to join the band in California. When she realized that Bo would not leave Bay St. Louis, Miss Dee returned instead to sing with Bo on the Mississippi Gulf Coast. They were married and have been together ever since.

With the advent of Elvis and others in the mid- to late '50s, local bands began to form to play rock 'n' roll at sock hops, school dances, graduation parties and other events. The most popular band in Gulfport was Johnny Elmer and the Rockets. In 1958, Johnny Elmer, whose father owned Elmer's Menswear in downtown Gulfport, formed the band with himself as the leader and founding member. Byron Brousard played the sax, and his brother Ronald "Boz" Broussard played the piano. Kenny Rich also played sax. Ray Dubuisson was on trumpet. Richard Fortner played guitar, and the band's vocalist was Salvadore "Penue" Taranto, who also played an upright bass.

Over time, the band members shifted and changed as some left for other bands or dropped out altogether. When Boz Broussard went off to college at Notre Dame, Walter Blessey from Biloxi replaced him. Walter only played with the Rockets for a short time before also going off to college at Ole Miss. The third piano player to join the Rockets was Hugh Beverly "Bev" Anderson.

Bev explained how he became a member of the band. His mother was a classically trained pianist who gave private piano lessons in Gulfport, so Bev had a basic knowledge of the instrument. After hearing Fats Domino in the early '50s, he was captivated by his style and would try to pick out some of

Johnny Elmer and the Rockets. *Left to right*: Sal "Penue" Taranto (upright bass, vocals), Richard Fortner (guitar), Walter Blessey (piano), Johnny Elmer (drums), Byron Broussard (alto sax), Ray Dubuisson (trumpet) and Kenny Rich (tenor sax). *From Bev Anderson.*

the chord structures on his mother's piano at home. He was surprised one day when Johnny Elmer, Ray Dubuisson and Penue Taranto showed up at his house. They said they were looking for a piano player. Penue said, "Hey, man, play me some Professor Longhair." Bev said he plunked around on the piano a bit, thinking he surely had failed the audition, but when he finished, Penue said, "Hey, man, you're hired."

Bev joined the band, and during practices, Richard Fortner, the guitar player, would show him some chord structures, which Bev picked up easily. Once he got started, he never stopped, and Bev is still playing with various groups on the coast.

Bev Anderson now plays occasionally with a band called the Checkmates. They have played regularly for several years at the French Club next to the Palace Casino in Biloxi. Sometimes the group is called the Out-Patient Band.

The Checkmates. *From Bev Anderson.*

Members of this incarnation of the Personalities are, *from left*, Joe "Big" Maurice (guitar), Ken Harder Jr. (sax), Sal "Penue" Taranto (vocals) and Bill Davis (trumpet). *From Bev Anderson.*

Another group that played on the coast, mostly at the Old Biloxi Hotel, was the Personalities. The group was made up of musicians from other bands who would come together and yet remained members of their regular bands.

During the late '50s, there were no elaborate sound systems. Many of the bands at the time still played hollow-body instruments like the guitar that Elvis made famous and the upright bass that Penue played in the early Rockets. The singer's microphone was run through the same amps as the guitar to provide a makeshift means for the vocalist to be heard over the instruments.

Johnny Elmer and the Rockets played music that was popular in New Orleans and throughout south Louisiana. Some songs that were standard at our dances were Bobby Charles's "On Bended Knee," Earl King's "Lonely, Lonely Nights," Jimmy Clanton's "Just a Dream" and Larry Williams's "Slow Down." The "jailhouse blues" style of Fats Domino had a big influence on many of the coast bands. His most notable characteristic was the use of piano triplets, influenced by Little Willie Littlefield. Littlefield had popularized the triplet beat on his initial recording, "It's Midnight." Domino's steady, hard-driving beat was stronger than boogie woogie or rhythm and blues and would become identified as the Fats Domino sound.

In 1949, Fats and his producer, Dave Bartholomew, took an old standard by New Orleans great Champion Jack Dupree called "Junker's Blues" and cleaned up the drug-focused lyrics to create Domino's first hit, "The Fat Man." The record also established his "wah-wah" vocal chorus that he would sing over his rolling piano bridge, a technique he used on several of his early records. He eventually discarded the style as his voice deepened with age.

The Domino beat was infectious, but it was the Cajun lilt to his voice that added the special touch to his recordings. It was this same Cajun accent that highlighted many of the swamp pop hits so popular in south Louisiana, East Texas and along the Mississippi Gulf Coast. Songs like Jivin' Gene's "Breaking Up Is Hard to Do," Rod Barnard's "This Should Go on Forever" and Joe Barry's "I'm a Fool to Care" would define the style that was inspired by Fats Domino.

One Gulfport musician became a cult figure in the swamp pop genre, not only because of his talent but also due to the tragedy of his lifestyle and eventual suicide. James Kenneth Donley was born and raised in Gulfport but was drawn to the New Orleans music scene at an early age. He quit school at sixteen and was working on the docks at the port of Gulfport but knew music was his calling. He began singing in the bars and clubs along the coast, imitating the sliding Cajun accent that is typical of swamp pop artists. His accent became so authentic it was hard to imagine that he had not grown up in that Cajun culture. He even used Fats's wah-wah style in some of his recordings. Donley had several

Jimmy Donley.

Jimmy Donley with Fats Domino.

close calls with success but could never quite achieve for himself what his songs did for other people. He eventually developed a friendship with his idol, Fats Domino, and would sell a song to him for as little as fifty dollars when Jimmy needed quick cash. Fats recorded seven of Jimmy's songs, including "What a Price," "Stop the Clock," "Bad Luck and Trouble" and "I've Been Calling." Since he sold the complete rights to his songs, his name does not appear as the writer on most of the labels. But Jimmy did have one hit on his own that would ultimately define his life. "Born to Be a Loser" became his only success. It was later covered by Jerry

Lee Lewis. Some of Jimmy Donley's more notable songs are "Please Mr. Sandman" and a great Christmas song, "Santa Don't Pass Me By." As Johnnie Allan and Bernice Larson Webb wrote in their biography of Jimmy, *Born to Be a Loser: The Story of a Rock 'n' Roll Poet's Tragic Life* (Jadfel, 1992), Jimmy Donley was certainly a loser who, as they said, "wrote songs in the key of heartbreak."

Another local musician who developed during the late '50s was Bob Morrison from Biloxi. His story of success is quite the opposite of Jimmy Donley's tragic tale. Bob, who was a gifted athlete as well as an accomplished guitarist, was exposed to several genres of music when he was young. His father, who supplied records to jukeboxes in the area, would bring home boxes of records that included pop, country and rhythm and blues. Bob developed a great ear for identifying hits, often giving his father tips as to what records should be loaded on the jukeboxes.

Bob was not only talented, but he was also smart. I first encountered Bob when we were engineering students at Mississippi State University. He graduated with a degree in nuclear engineering while I was studying electrical engineering. I was a novice guitar player during that period, and several of us would hang out in Bob's room to hear him play such pop songs as "Moonlight in Vermont" and throbbing guitar hits like Link Wray's "Rumble." We were fascinated by his knowledge of music and could only hope to master the guitar chords he would show us.

While in college, he began playing area clubs and developed a following over on the West Coast as well. After signing a contract with Columbia Records, he moved to California, where he also tried his hand at acting. After a brief stint in Hollywood, he moved to Nashville, where he began writing songs for others. His first hit was "The River's Too Wide," recorded by Olivia Newton-John. He went on to write or co-write "Angels, Roses and Rain," recorded by Dickie Lee; "Midnight Angel" by Barbara Mandrell; and "Up to Heaven," which became the first hit for Reba McEntire. Bob won several awards, including ASCAP's Songwriter of the Year in 1978, 1980, 1981 and 1982. In 1979, he received a Grammy along with his co-writer, Debbie Hupp, for the Kenny Rogers hit "You Decorated My Life."

There were several other bands that played in the '50s on the Gulf Coast. The Rockin' Rebels in Biloxi became as popular as Johnny Elmer and the Rockets in Gulfport. Ray Fournier, one of the founding members of the Rockin' Rebels, explained how the band was formed. He and some friends were regulars at the Slovenian Lodge on the corner of Myrtle and

1ˢᵗ Streets. One day, some of the people at the Lodge were trying to put together entertainment for the weekend and told Ray and the others that they ought to put a band together. It sounded like a good idea, so Ray, along with Bun Blessey, Penue Taranto and others, formed the Rockin' Rebels and began performing at the Slovenian Lodge. When Penue, their lead singer, left the Rebels to join Johnny Elmer in Gulfport, the band suggested that Fournier, who had been singing background with the group, take over as the new lead singer. Ray remembers going home to his mother and telling her that he was the new lead singer of the Rockin' Rebels. She shrugged it off and said, "What were they thinking, Ray, you can't sing." But sing he did, and he continues to be a popular singer in Biloxi today. His recording of "Cherry Pie" became the preferred version of the song along the coast. Marvin and Johnny, a Los Angeles–based doowop duo, had originally recorded the song in 1954. "Cherry Pie" was a big seller, due in part to its double-entendre lyrics. The song was later revived by Skip and Flip in 1960, but Ray's local version remains the favorite along the coast.

A band called the Personalities also played on the coast. The band was made up of various musicians from other bands who would come together

The Rocking Rebels. *From Bev Anderson.*

as a group. Different players would rotate through the band at various times. The band is best remembered as a regular at the old Biloxi Hotel.

Garland Moran and the Night Travelers is a family band that has been around for fifty-plus years. The band consisted of Garland and his brothers, Gayle and Perry Moran. Their father, Olige Moran, played the fiddle and could play just about any of the other instruments as well. Olige had started the boys playing guitar when they were very young. They were already performing in public before they were in their teens. As they got older, they formed the Night Travelers and played all over the coast. Not only did they play at the World's Fair in New Orleans, but they were also the closing band every year for at least fifty years at the Deep-Sea Fishing Rodeo in Gulfport. Along with the brothers, a couple of additional musicians would play with them, often an uncle or a cousin. For that reason, they were also known simply as the Moran Family Band.

While rock 'n' roll seemed to dominate the music scene in Gulfport in the 1950s, there were other styles of popular music still on the charts. Songs like "Old Cape Cod," by Patti Page, "Dark Moon" by Gale Storm, "Catch a Falling Star" by Perry Como, "On the Street Where You Live" by Vic Damone and Patti Page's "How Much Is that Doggie in the Window?" competed with rock 'n' roll music for positions on the pop charts. The smooth style of these songs was still popular even as the transition to the more youth-oriented music began to occur.

In the late 1950s, Karl and Joe Fasold and Aubrey Marshal were enjoying a coffee break at the Dog House Jr. on 14th Street. The conversation turned to music, and before long, the concept of a dance band began to take shape. The men recognized a need in Gulfport for a more mature sound for formal dances, carnival balls, conventions, yacht club parties and other private functions. From their initial discussion, the three musicians went on to form the Skyliners, which would become one of the leading dance bands in Gulfport and along the coast. The members of the band were Charlie Kennedy on piano, Aubrey on drums, Karl on alto sax, Jerry Bienvenu also on alto sax, Joe Fasold on tenor sax, Harold Lizare on bass and Don Dubuisson on trombone. Betty Rogers was the vocalist for the Skyliners but only joined the group for larger events at places like the Keesler Officers' Club, formal dances and conventions at the Broadwater Beach Hotel and various charity balls on the coast. The Skyliners disbanded after the devastation of Hurricane Camille in 1969 and only got back together to play the New Year's Eve party at the Hattiesburg Country Club in 1970 and 1971, which would prove to be their last engagement.

The original Skyliners orchestra: Charlie Kennedy (piano), Aubrey Marshal (drums), Harold Lizare (bass), Karl Fasold (alto sax), Jerry Bienvenu (alto sax), Richard Johnson (tenor sax), Joe Fasold (trumpet) and Don Dubuisson (trombone). *From Karl Fasold.*

Bob Slade Orchestra. *From the Slade family.*

The Slade Brothers Orchestra from Lumberton, Mississippi, was another popular big-band group that played at various clubs and events in Gulfport in the 1940s and 1950s. There were fourteen children in the Slade family. All were musically talented, and each had learned to play more than one instrument, all by ear. The boys formed the Slade Brothers Orchestra in the late '40s and were soon in demand all over the coast at places like the Merry Mansion, the Broadwater Beach Hotel, Porter's restaurant and lounge, the Silver Moon Club on Highway 49 and the Golden Rod club on Reynoir Street in Biloxi.

The orchestra consisted of brothers Bob, Bernard "Bernie," J.R., Munch and Guy Slade. Scooter Whatley from Pascagoula was the only member of the band who was not a relative. Bob Slade, who preferred playing Dixieland jazz to the big-band music of his brothers, eventually left to form his own group, the Bob Slade Orchestra. Bob also played jazz piano as an individual performer at various clubs on the strip. The brothers continued to play big-band music under the original family name, the Slade Brothers Orchestra, well into the '60s.

Slade Brothers Orchestra. *From the Slade family.*

Bernie Slade's daughter described the brothers as handsome and always well dressed. Her father played the drums and the stand-up bass; he would play an impromptu tune made up for his family just before leaving the house for a gig. His daughter also recalled how she and the other children were allowed to attend the Christmas party every year at the Edgewater Gulf Hotel where the Slade Brothers Orchestra was the featured band. She would dress up for the occasion and feel like royalty. She fondly recalls that the last event the Slade Brothers Orchestra played was at her wedding reception on August 7, 1976. It was a bittersweet moment for all, since her father and uncle J.R. were the only Slades left in the band at that time.

The many clubs and hotels along the beach in Gulfport and Biloxi were steppingstones for up-and-coming musicians. In addition to Elvis, Jerry Lee Lewis, Fats Domino, Jimmy Reed, Roosevelt Sykes, Slim Harpo, Hank Williams and others who played on the Gulf Coast when they were just starting their careers, local artists like Jimmy Donley, Bob Morrison and, later, Jimmy Buffett had varying degrees of national success. The music and culture of New Orleans and the Gulf Coast were intertwined, helping to shape the underlying fabric that was Gulfport during its golden era.

Chapter 7

LET'S GO TO THE HOP

*7*he advent of rock 'n' roll brought about dramatic changes in our music and the way we danced. The swing era that had dominated the '30s and '40s was coming to an end as the large dance bands downsized to smaller nightclub acts with featured vocalists.

The strong backbeat of rock 'n' roll required a different style of dancing. It was also clear we just didn't want to dance the way our parents danced, particularly since they were so opposed to our new music. At first, all of the teen dances were called "the bop." The words *bop* and *bebop* were new, having developed from the new jazz styles of the mid-'40s, so *bop* was used to refer to all the new dance moves. Although most of our dances in Gulfport were still swing-based, different styles developed throughout the country. These differences were brought together in unified styles that were popularized on the television show *American Bandstand*, hosted by Dick Clark. The dances that had developed regionally suddenly became national fads as we watched and learned the moves from the teens on the show.

At first, the music of the previous generation was still evident in the early stages of rock 'n' roll. Even some of the pioneers of our music recorded hits in the old swing style. Elvis recorded, almost word for word, "Are You Lonesome Tonight," originally by Al Jolson. Jerry Lee Lewis had a hit with "Crazy Arms" by country legend Ray Price. Little Richard's record "Baby Face," originally a hit for Jan Garber, peaked at number twelve on the R&B charts. And Fats Domino recorded several classics such as "My Blue Heaven," "Margie" and "Red Sails in the Sunset."

"Sock hops," "record hops" or simply just "hops" became the name for our informal dances. The teen dances throughout the country were typically held in school gymnasiums or cafeterias. To avoid damaging the varnished gym floors, dancers were required to remove their hard-soled shoes. This led to the name "sock hops" and the term "bobby soxers," referring to teenagers. Music was often provided by disc jockeys playing 45 rpm records, although in Gulfport there were usually performances by live bands like Bo and Dee, the Claudetts, Johnny Elmer and the Rockets or Ray Fournier and the Rocking Rebels.

In 1957, the vocal group Danny and the Juniors had a number-one record called "At the Hop" with lyrics that called out many of the popular dances of the day, as well as naming our dance locations as "the hop."

Our dances in Gulfport were generally held in the B. Frank Brown Memorial Gymnasium across the street from the high school, the old yacht club or the West Side Community Center. Our dances were most often sponsored by the school and were chaperoned by teachers or parents.

Sock hops were not just for dancing; they were really all about socializing. They provided an opportunity to just hang out with a date or mingle with friends. For the dances, girls wore sweaters with circle skirts. The hems of

Gulfport High School. *Paul Jermyn collection.*

B. Frank Brown Gymnasium. *From Glen East, Gulfport Separate School District superintendent.*

The Yacht Club. *Paul Jermyn collection.*

the skirts were cut just below the knees to make it easier to perform the kicks and jumps of the various dance moves. The skirts often sported the image of a cuddly animal. The most popular was the poodle skirt, which became an iconic symbol of the rockin' '50s. The guys were more casual, usually wearing only a white T-shirt and slacks. As Boyd Bennett said on his hit record "Black Slacks," "When you put 'em on you were ready to go." Depending on how we chose to dress up the look, a boy could appear to be a clean-cut boy next door or a "hood" with a pack of cigarettes rolled up in his sleeve.

Like other fads, new dances came and went, although some basic moves like the jive or jitterbug are still around today. The popularity of most dances only lasted for a while, but they were around long enough to become part of our teenage years. Here are some dances that were popular in Gulfport in the '50s.

THE BOP

"Bop" was a general term that included many of the dances that were popular in the '50s. It was a lot like the jive or swing, but the couples did not hold hands.

THE BUNNY HOP

The bunny hop was a conga-style line dance created in 1952 by the students at Balboa High School in San Francisco. Big band leader Ray Anthony wrote and recorded a hit record inspired by the dance. The bunny hop is considered a party dance because of the fun interaction with the dancers in the group.

THE HOKEY POKEY

The "Hokey Pokey," another dance classic, became popular in the '50s as the B-side of Ray Anthony's record "The Bunny Hop." The song was much like a square dance with a caller calling out the dance moves. Jo Ann Greer was the singer on Anthony's record who sang the moves for the dancers to make.

THE STROLL

The stroll is one of the more popular and identifiable dances of the '50s. The kids on *American Bandstand* created the dance after hearing the song "C.C. Rider" by Chuck Willis. With the success of the bunny hop and the hokey pokey, they began to create new dances for any new beat that was popular. The stroll was one of those dances.

To do the stroll, we lined up facing each other, with the boys on one side and girls on the other with a wide space between the two lines. The boy and girl at the head of the line would begin by coming together and doing a shuffle-type step down the middle, showing off their moves while those in line waited their turn. After that couple reached the end of the line, the next couple would start down the middle.

Songs like "Rumble" by Link Wray, "Stroll Me" by Kay Starr and "Rock and Stroll Room" by Mickey and Sylvia had the perfect sliding beat for the stroll. Chuck Willis was so identified with the dance that he became known as the "King of the Stroll." The dance was so popular that Dick Clark approached the Diamonds to write a song especially for the dance. The Diamonds, whose hit "Little Darlin'" was then currently at the top of the charts, took Clark's suggestion. They wrote and recorded "The Stroll," which immediately went gold and defined the dance.

THE HAND JIVE

In 1958, the record "Willy and the Hand Jive" by Johnny Otis was at the top of the charts. It remained at the top for sixteen astonishing weeks. The hand jive was a dance that mostly incorporated hand movements in a systematic pattern. The dance could even be done sitting down.

THE MADISON

The Madison started in the late '50s and became really popular in 1960. Dancers danced in a group similar to our current line dances like the electric slide. It was also similar to square dances, in which the artist called out a series of dance moves with specific steps. The hit record that gave rise to the dance was "The Madison" by Al Brown's Tunetoppers. There was a competing record by Ray Bryant called "Madison Time," which was almost identical. Some of the steps called on both records were "The Double Cross," "The Big M," "The Jackie Gleason," "The Rifleman" and "Two Up and Two Back," just to name a few.

THE CHA-CHA

The cha-cha was created in the late '40s during a time in America when Latin rhythms were becoming very popular. But it didn't really become popular until the '50s. The dancers incorporated a triple step that created a cha-cha-cha sound when their shoes hit the floor. The name of the dance derived from the sound. Our parents seemed to enjoy the cha-cha more than we ever did. They danced the mambo, the tango and the cha-cha at clubs like the Broadwater Beach and the Fiesta.

Several artists released records in an attempt to cash in on the cha-cha craze, but few of them had any significant rise on the charts. There was "Tea for Two Cha Cha" by Tommy Dorsey in 1958 and "Everybody Loves to Cha Cha" by Sam Cooke in 1959. Johnny Otis recorded "Willy Did the Cha Cha" in 1958, in an attempt to revive the amazing success of his previous hit, "Willy and the Hand Jive," but the song was barely noticed.

THE MAMBO

A Cuban composer created mambo music in the 1930s, but it was not until the late 1940s that another Cuban, Perez Prado, created a dance to go along with the music. In 1950, American bandleader Sonny Burke brought Prado's music to America with his recording of "Mambo Jambo." The mambo became another popular Latin dance craze during the mid-'50s in part because of Perez Prado. The dance could be described as having freedom of movement with complicated footwork.

Perez Prado, who was known as the Mambo King, had several mambo records on the Billboard charts. Prado's "Cherry Pink and Apple Blossom White" was a huge hit in 1955 featuring an unforgettable trumpet solo by Billy Regis. Prado followed that hit with "Patricia" in 1958. The pulsating organ on the record made "Patricia" a popular song for skating at Mrs. Rippy's skating rink in Gulfport.

Other artists had mambo hits, including "Mardi Gras Mambo" by the Hawketts, who later became famous as the Neville Brothers of New Orleans. Various pop singers also had mambo hits in 1954, including Perry Como with "Papa Loves Mambo" and Rosemary Clooney with "Mambo Italiano." Big-band singer Vaughn Monroe joined the mambo craze with "They Were Doin' the Mambo."

According to Norm N. Nite's book *Rock On*, today the mambo dance is different from the version of the 1940s and 1950s and is now generally known as salsa.

THE TWIST

The twist was the most popular dance of the '50s and early '60s. Written and recorded in 1958 by Hank Ballard and the Midnighters, the song was later recorded by Chubby Checker in 1960, and it rushed to the top of the charts. Dick Clark's wife gave Chubby Checker his name as a take-off of Fats Domino. Checker's version of the "Twist" became so popular that he created the dance to go along with the song.

In 1961, Cholly Knickerbocker, a columnist with the *Journal American*, happened to see Prince Serge Obolensky doing the twist at the Peppermint Lounge in New York. Obolensky was a Russian American aristocrat, U.S. Army paratrooper, socialite and publicist. Knickerbocker reported what she saw, and society picked up on it. Apparently, the elite felt that if Obolensky was dancing the twist, there must be something to it.

For several months, celebrities like Jackie Kennedy, Liberace, Truman Capote, John Wayne and Nat "King" Cole danced the twist at the Peppermint Lounge. Joey Dee and the Starliters, the house band at the club, became so popular that they released their own recording called "The Peppermint Twist" in honor of the club. Their song replaced Checker's version on the top spot in 1961. The twist continued to be popular, and Chubby Checker's song reached the number-one spot again in 1962. According to Billboard, it is the only record to ever reach number one in two different years.

ROCK 'N' ROLL

Music was changing by the end of the '50s, which meant the dances were also changing. Partners no longer held each other but rather moved to the beat of the music on their own. Dances that had been popular since the advent of rock 'n' roll gave way to the new dance fads of the '60s, such as the twist and the locomotion. Other dances that quickly came and went were the pony, the alligator, the monkey, the sweet pea, the Watusi, the fly, the slop and the fish. Many of these songs were mentioned in Chris Kenner's song "Land of a Thousand Dances," also a hit for Cannibal and the Headhunters in 1965.

Chapter 8

WATCHING THE SUBMARINE RACES

*W*e were different from past generations because of the freedoms we enjoyed. This new independence allowed us to redefine the way things were done in America. Dating was one of the traditions that we revolutionized. Although we did not know we were doing so at the time, we were actually changing the rules of "going out" while forming the basis of what teenagers consider normal today.

Dating as we know it is exclusive to American culture. Few other countries have the social conditions that would allow them to pursue the practice with the same intensity as we are able to enjoy. In other parts of the world, boys and girls attend separate schools and have far stricter rules of society.

Before World War II, a man in the United States called on a woman with the idea of possible marriage. In the '50s, this was not the primary goal. We dated because it was fun and it allowed us to interact with the opposite sex without our parents meddling. Although people dated before the 1950s, after the '50s, dating became more popular and routine. It was common for us to go out on a date one or more times a week. We also started dating younger than the previous generation. In fact, a girl who had not started dating by the age of thirteen or so was considered a "late bloomer."

Dating went through a series of phases as we grew into our teen years. As preteens, we never had the slightest thoughts or understanding of any romantic relationships. As we got older, flirting eventually led to dating. Some of us began by double dating, since the whole idea of "going out" on a date was rather awkward. Double dating made for easy conversation, since the couples were probably good friends anyway.

Blind dates were another acceptable way to meet someone. But with a blind date, there was always a risk. Theoretically, a blind date should be a good thing, but it didn't always work out that way. There was a 50/50 chance that there just wasn't any chemistry between the two or that one of the persons turned out to be a real "basket case."

Eventually, there was single dating, and while it got easier after a while, it was still awkward at times. Asking a girl out for the first time has always been stressful. Even the most experienced boy would often find himself going over and over in his head what he was going to say when "she" answered the phone, particularly if the girl was someone he found super attractive. When we finally got up the nerve to dial her number, we were always "bummed out" when the girl's mother answered the phone, and we would just simply "corrode" if her father ever answered first.

If a relationship grew after a number of dates, we began "going steady." Going steady took on a whole new meaning for us in the '50s. Before the war, going steady was more serious. For us, it only meant that we were obliged to date each other exclusively. We had an understanding that we belonged to each other, but only for the purpose of dating. We went steady without any real thoughts of marriage. Of course, there were a few exceptions, but they were hardly the rule.

There were certain expectations for those who went steady. It was more or less expected that the boy would give the girl something like his class ring, a letter jacket or an ID bracelet to show to everyone that they were attached. The girl would often wear the boy's ring on a chain around her neck, but most chose to wear it on their hands. The ring was worn on the third finger of her left hand and usually required string wrapped around the back of the ring and painted with clear nail polish to adjust the size. The use of a real ring guard to make the boy's ring fit her smaller finger was the "coolest."

Boys were expected to call their steady girlfriends a certain number of times during the week and to take them out on a certain number of dates. Going steady reduced the anxiety about dating that most teenagers experienced and also provided a certain degree of security for the couple. Having a steady boyfriend or girlfriend assured we would have a date to all the important social functions like the senior high prom. There was so much pressure on teenagers that girls would often drive through Park & Eat or Parkside on Saturday afternoon with their hair in bouffant curlers to give the impression that they were getting ready for a date later on in the evening, even if they may be facing the weekend alone.

Although the '50s were still somewhat prudish, going steady also meant that the couple could go a step beyond what was normally acceptable intimacy for a regular date. This caused much anxiety for the parents who were understandably concerned that so much close contact with only one person would encourage "going all the way."

By the time we were in high school, it was not uncommon to see kissing, hugging and other mild forms of affection in public. We weren't self-conscious to kiss or hug in the hallway at school, at ballgames, at the beach and definitely not in our cars. Although we didn't actually call it "necking" and "petting," we knew what the terms meant, and it was almost expected on most dates. "Heavy petting," on the other hand, took it one step further and was very close to "doing it."

In the '50s, our automobiles provided the perfect opportunity for dating couples to play around. There was just the right amount of privacy for sexual experimentation. Cars were like apartments on wheels. The privacy that our automobiles provided ensured that we could "make out" without interruption.

Our parents knew we were "parking" but really had no effective way to prevent it. There were several secluded sites along the coast where we could pull our cars away from the normal traffic to sneak some time together. The most popular place for parking with the Gulfport crowd was not one of those hidden-away places but rather one that was right in plain sight on busy Highway 90. In fact, sometimes it was so crowded that it was difficult to find an empty space. "The Rock Pile" was the place almost everyone went to park at one time or another. Located at the south end of Court House Road and Highway 90 in what was then Mississippi City, it still exists today.

When the sun went down, cars would gradually begin to arrive. Couples would find their favorite spot from which to watch "the submarine races," the '50s term for making out in our cars. For those who cared to notice, the moon appeared to hang in the sky, forming a road of light on the rippling dark waters. The Rock Pile was quite romantic, although romance really had nothing to do with it.

Girls who found themselves without a date on Saturday night had an alternative that many actually looked forward to: a "slumber party." The girls would get together, put their hair up in rollers, play with their makeup, talk and giggle about boys and listen to 45 rpm records, all while munching on their favorite snacks. All of this would go on late into the night, until they would finally give up and fall asleep. Sometimes they would make "love chains" by folding chewing gum wrappers. This "make-him-love-me" craze was one of the fun things to do when they got together. To make the magic work, the girl created the chain as long as her intended boyfriend was tall. Burning the chain was supposed to ensure an eventual romance.

In Gulfport during the '50s, we had many options for places to go and things to do on a date. The most popular places were of course the movies and drive-in restaurants like the White Cap, Park & Eat and Parkside. We would often cruise through these popular meeting places several times in a night, just to see who was "hanging out."

We also lived in a time when illegal gambling and lax enforcement of the drinking laws were the norm on the coast. The White Cap Drive-in on the beach in Mississippi City was a popular hangout that offered curb service like the other drive-in restaurants, but at the White Cap, we

White Cap Drive-In.

could purchase mixed drinks from a carhop without getting out of our cars and without ever being asked for an ID. Mississippi City was not part of municipal Gulfport at the time and therefore not subject to city laws. Many of us had our first taste of alcohol at the White Cap, most likely a rum and Coke.

We could also buy liquor by the bottle at some of the honkytonks on old Highway 49. The more adventurous of us would head north out of the city limits past the Milk of Magnesia plant to the string of black clubs that lined the highway. We first came to the Silver Moon Club, and then farther up on the right were the Cotton Club and the Hi Hat Club. Across the highway on the left were the Evangeline Club and the Beverly Lounge, followed by the Barn located next to the Turkey Creek Bridge. Those who had qualms about going in the black clubs could drive up to a side window and purchase a bottle of liquor without an ID and without getting out of their cars.

Drive-in movies were called "passion pits."

We often absentmindedly drove off with the speakers still attached to our cars.

Dates were expensive, even if it was only for the movies, popcorn and a Coke, especially if we dated frequently. The idea of going "Dutch" was not acceptable, so the boy was expected to pay for everything. According to *Seventeen* magazine, in 1959, a typical boy would spend an average of $7.00 per month on dates. The amount would increase if there were any special events, such as a birthday that required a gift or a Saturday night dance that required a corsage. Flowers were an additional expense that ranged from $1.50 to $10.00, depending on the kind of flowers. Orchids, which were the most popular corsages, cost about $7.00 per flower. Tuxedo rental, costing about $10.00, was another expense boys faced for formal dances. Although the boy bore the basic cost of the date, girls also had expenses. A dress for a prom or formal would cost anywhere from $15.00 to $45.00. Then they had to purchase shoes and a handbag to match, which could add upward of $10.00 to the total. As it turns out, the girls spent more on their proms and formals than the boys did.

We also enjoyed taking our dates to the "picture show," and in the '50s, there were many teen-oriented movies. Movies allowed us to sit in the dark with our date, enjoy popcorn or candy and also be entertained. If you took your date to a drive-in movie, or "passion pit" as we called them, you could often be entertained without ever watching the show.

Chapter 9

RESTAURANTS, CLUBS AND FAMILY ATTRACTIONS

*G*oing out to eat in Gulfport in the '50s was generally reserved for special occasions. Family budgets were too tight for eating out on a regular basis. Since our mothers prepared most of the family meals, the food industry began to target this group. They began producing a whole array of new and convenient products in the form of canned goods, frozen foods, boxed mixes and prepared snacks. These easy-to-prepare meals lined the shelves of supermarkets like the Be-Wise on 25th Avenue and the Jitney-Jungle on Pass Road. Eventually, we began to look not so much for nourishment but for convenience.

A popular new feature was the recipes that appeared on the backs of cans and boxes. The most innovative and successful recipe appeared in 1954 on the back of a Lipton's box of dehydrated onion soup. By adding the soup powder to ordinary sour cream, a delicious dip was created. Originally called "California Dip," it became known simply as "French Onion Dip." By using potato chips as a scoop, the chip and dip was born. Following the success of Lipton's, other dips have been created, but the original onion dip remains the most popular today.

Eating meals at home was a family affair. Most of us sat down for meals together. The children were expected to help serve and to clean up afterward. There were no special menus or diets. We all ate the same food, and we were expected to "clean our plates."

By the late '50s, as the economy continued to improve, we began to eat out more often. The ambiance of the restaurant became important, and we chose restaurants that had just the right atmosphere. We liked looking out at the water, whether it was overlooking the Gulf at Baricev's or Back Bay at Popps Ferry. We also chose restaurants for their specialties, such as down-home cooking at the Friendship House or Italian food at Angelo's.

There were several iconic eating places that we all enjoyed. The following is a partial list of some of our favorite eating places.

FAVORITE RESTAURANTS AND EATING SPOTS

Stone's Ice Cream Parlor

Dan Stone opened the Stone's Ice Cream Parlor at 2215 14th Street in 1937 and was Gulfport's answer to the classic '50s malt shop. Stone's was the favorite hangout for students, families and businessmen throughout its long history. On

Dan and Carroll Stone in front of their prized refrigerator truck, 1945. *From the Stone Sisters.*

Sundays, families would drive around, ending up at Stone's for an afternoon treat. After the movies, students on dates would walk or drive to Stone's for an end to the evening. After lunch, businessmen and students would stop by Stone's before returning to the office or school. Stone's Ice Cream made a wide variety of unique flavors. Some of the most requested flavors were orange pineapple, grape pineapple, pecan crunch and peach.

Pop Corn King

Almost everyone in Gulfport knew Clarence Welch, the "Pop Corn King." One of his fruit-flavored snowballs was a must on our hot summer days. His peanuts and popcorn were standards served from his white food truck at every sporting event.

Clarence Welch, the "Pop Corn King." *From Debra Reyer Hilton.*

Simmons' Park & Eat Drive-In. *Clayton Rand Papers, Manuscripts Division, Special Collections Department, Mississippi State University Libraries.*

Simmons' Park & Eat

The Park & Eat was one of our favorite hangouts. Owned and operated by well-known coast restaurateur Jack Simmons, the drive-in focused on curb service. We would pull up and park with our music blaring and were quickly greeted by a carhop to take our orders. Unlike the classic drive-ins of the movies, the carhops at the Park & Eat didn't wear roller skates, but the service was just as fast. Drive-in restaurants developed out of our passion for speed and efficiency. The idea was convenient for the customers, but it was also a cost-effective concept for the owners. Whether after school or on a Saturday night date, a stop at the Park & Eat was a must for our favorite hamburger, fries and a Barq's root beer.

Sinopoli's Parkside Drive-In

In the '50s, Jack Simmons and Himbert Sinopoli took over the popular but small Pam's Drive-In from owner Jack Beattle. Located at the intersection of 38th Avenue and Highway 90, the restaurant was named after Beattle's

Pam's Drive-In later became Sinopoli's Parkside. *Paul Jermyn collection.*

sister, Pam. Sinopoli changed the name to Parkside and ran the drive-in that was similar to Jack Simmons' Park & Eat on the beach in Gulfport. Later, Himbert and his brother, Charlie, took over the Parkside Drive-In from Simmons and turned it into one of our favorite cruising places. We drove through Parkside several times in one night just to check out our friends. No evening was complete without a pink lemonade and a steak sandwich at Parkside.

Hugo's Pizza

Hugo's Pizza at the corner of Porter Avenue and West Division Street in Biloxi was the most popular pizza restaurant on the coast in the '50s and '60s. Hugo Joseph Rungo Sr., a native of New York stationed at Keesler, opened Hugo's in 1951. It had a great Italian ambiance with red-and-white checkered tablecloths, wine bottle candleholders with wax dripping down the sides and a window through which you could watch the cooks sling the pizza dough by hand. The coast tradition of eating French dressing on pizza began at Hugo's and quickly became a fad all over the area. Called "liquid cheese" by the locals, it was actually French dressing, more specifically the Catalina brand. The dressing was served at the tables in the same kinds of squeeze bottles that held the mayonnaise, mustard and catsup. There are various stories as to how and when this tradition started, but many of us still squirt French dressing on our pizzas today. Hugo's closed its doors in 2003.

The Dog House Jr.

Located on 14th Street between 26th and 27th Avenues in downtown Gulfport, the Dog House Jr. was one of the most popular fast-food places in the '50s. It featured what many considered the best chili dogs, chili cheeseburgers and hamburgers. The building was very small, measuring about six feet by ten feet, and only had room for six customers inside. There were no tables, only wooden barstools at the counter. During peak hours, there was always a line of people waiting their turn to get in. There was a walk-up window in the alley on the side of the building where we could place and pick up our orders.

Angelo's Place

Angelo's Place on Highway 90 in Gulfport was probably the most famous and endearing restaurant on the Gulf Coast. It was owned and operated by Angelo Xidis, who emigrated from Greece at the age of sixteen. After moving to Gulfport in 1935, he started a small diner. As his business grew, so did the diner, until it became the fine building made of steel and glass that we all knew. Since Angelo was not sure if his restaurant would survive the numerous hurricanes, he built his additions over the years around the large oak trees that were on the property. His decision not to cut them down was a brilliant marketing move, since all of his patrons enjoyed the novel décor. Only at Angelo's Place could you relish your meal inside while sitting under live oak trees.

Patrons dined on such delicacies as Italian spaghetti a la Caruso, pan-roasted scallops and oysters, broiled flounder with Angelo's special lemon oil sauce, chicken livers à la Milanese and spaghetti with meatballs. One of the specialties was stuffed flounder covered in Mister Xidis's special garlic tomato sauce. Angelo guarded his unique recipes closely, even keeping the formulas secret from his employees.

Angelo's Place. *Paul Jermyn collection.*

Angelo Xidis cooking spaghetti. *Paul Jermyn collection.*

Baricev's Seafood Restaurant

Joseph Peter Baricev opened his first seafood restaurant in Biloxi after moving from New Orleans in the 1940s. The restaurant was destroyed in the 1947 hurricane but was rebuilt on the site across from the Buena Vista Hotel. The 3,500-square-foot building consisted of a lobby, the main dining room, a lounge off from the entrance, the kitchen off to the right where diners could watch men shucking oysters, restrooms and supply rooms. When Baricev died, his son Joseph Francis took over the business along with Joseph's brother and their wives. They turned Baricev's Seafood Restaurant into an institution famous for broiled stuffed flounder, rich gumbo and raw oysters, southern-style fried chicken, trout amandine, whole broiled lobster, crabmeat au gratin and broiled choice rib-eye steak with French fries, a green salad, hot rolls and butter. Although we thought of it as a seafood restaurant, it was really so much more.

Fisherman's Wharf

Although the Fisherman's Wharf did not open until the early '60s, it quickly became a coast favorite. Located across from Oak Street on the south side of Highway 90, the restaurant was owned and operated by the Ladner family. The whole concept of a fisherman's cabin was Ladner's wife's idea. She supervised the entire project, incorporating elements that would be reminiscent of a fishing hut. She introduced such features as finger bowls for keeping fingers fresh and using dish towels in place of napkins to enhance the rustic look. There was an oyster bar where patrons could watch employees shuck fresh oysters while enjoying a Barq's or a Dixie beer. The Ladners continued to run the restaurant until 1975, when they sold it to the Aldridge family. The Aldridge family introduced several of their own delicious recipes, including what eventually became the specialty of the house, the Fisherman's Wharf Pie, still talked about today.

The Friendship House Restaurant

Jim and Mary Meyers opened the Friendship House Restaurant in 1949. Their daughter, Susie Wilson, told the story that her father had been to the horse tracks in New Orleans and had won a large sum of money. He came back to Biloxi after his good fortune and bought the old Dinty Moore restaurant on the corner of DeBuys Road and Highway 90. He and Mary converted Dinty Moore's restaurant into the Friendship House. Located midway between Gulfport and Biloxi, it was advertised to be exactly six miles east of Gulfport and six miles west of Biloxi.

It was a great place for breakfast, served by waitresses in starched white uniforms with red trim, at tables overlooking the Gulf. The Friendship House was known as much for its great cup of coffee as any of its delicious items on the menu. Along with the basket of biscuits that was served at each table, Mary included her trademark plum jelly.

The Friendship House featured a "Hospitality Menu" every day from 11:30 a.m. to 3:00 p.m. Prices during that time were reduced on specialty items. Among the items offered were a cup of seafood gumbo for $0.35 or a flounder plate that included a flounder steak fried in cornmeal, French fried potatoes, green beans or peas, lettuce and tomato salad for only $1.25. For dessert, there was chocolate icebox pie covered with whipped cream or fresh baked apple pie for only $0.25. Other choices of entrées included broiled lobster, veal cutlet, short rib of beef, stuffed deviled crab, spaghetti, creamed

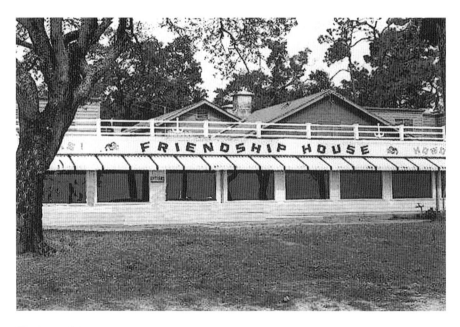

The Friendship House restaurant.

chicken, Swiss steak and roast loin of pork. All included delicious sides like candied sweet potatoes, homemade dressing, mashed potatoes with gravy and others.

The regular menu featured much of the same. Entrées included boneless sirloin prepared to choice, veal cutlet, fried chicken, Swiss steak with wine gravy, short rib of beef, spaghetti, creamed chicken and beef stew. The prices ranged from $1.25 to no more than $1.95, with the exception of the boneless sirloin, which was $5.75. A children's menu was available with most items.

The Friendship House was sold to the Brennan family from New Orleans in 1963. The Brennans ran the restaurant successfully until it finally closed in 1980.

Shortly after the Meyerses sold the Friendship House, they opened the Log Cabin restaurant a little bit north on DeBuys Road. It soon became just as popular, thanks to the great hospitality and good food served up by Jim and Mary Meyers.

Palm Drive-In

The Palm Drive-In was a white masonry block building on the southwest corner of 22nd Avenue and 22nd Street. It got its name from the few palm trees that surrounded the lot. The interior was plain, with only a few booths and a couple of the most popular pinball machines on the coast. Some would argue that the pinball machines kept the Palm Drive-In in business. Players had a better than even chance to win, and they would. The machines would regularly pay off a nickel for every game won. It was not unusual for someone to make a couple bucks.

Although the food was not particularly outstanding, it was good enough for many of us to keep going back for more. The oyster and shrimp po'boys were good, as were the roast beef po'boys. Some preferred the chili dogs, while others liked the Palm hamburgers. The beer was cold and inexpensive. For curb service, we would blink our headlights to signal for a carhop. Anything we wanted would be delivered directly to our cars.

Popps Ferry Restaurant

Popps Ferry was one of the best restaurants for informal dining on the Gulf Coast, not only recognized for its delicious menu but also the picturesque setting overlooking Biloxi's Back Bay. Located at the foot of the Popps Ferry Bridge, this popular eatery was owned by the Sinopoli brothers. Charlie Sinopoli had started in the restaurant business with the Dog House on Pass Road, which he had leased from well-known coast restaurateur Jack Simmons. Later, Charlie and his brother Himbert took over the Parkside Drive-In restaurant on the beach, also from Simmons. Their brother Raymond joined them, and the three bought the Popps Ferry Restaurant from J.N. Randall Sr.

The restaurant was known for its excellent food at reasonable prices. The Tuesday night "all you can eat" chicken special served family style was a favorite. Steak Night was on Thursdays, featuring ten different kinds of steaks, broiled any way the customer requested. On Friday nights, you could "eat your fill" of fried fish with salad, French fries and homemade buttermilk biscuits and plum preserves. On Sundays, the special was a turkey dinner, including corn bread dressing, giblet gravy, candied yams and cranberry sauce. All of these specials were only $1.25 per person and $0.75 for a child's plate. These were real bargains, even in the '50s.

After graduating from college, Gary Sinopoli joined his three brothers in their restaurant business, opening a Colonel Dixie in Picayune (1965) and on Courthouse Road in Gulfport (1966). Many remember the hamburgers and fries at Colonel Dixie that were only fifteen cents and the popular hot dogs that were served with chili and sauerkraut. The average check was usually less than seventy cents each.

Later, the brothers opened the extremely successful Catfish Charlie's, which featured fried catfish and the same buttermilk biscuits that were so popular at Popps Ferry Restaurant. You could be assured that if it was a Sinopoli restaurant, you received the best food at the best price.

FAVORITE NIGHTSPOTS

The Creole Room

The Creole Room was located inside the Biloxi Hotel to the left of the main lobby down a couple stairs into the lower level. Upon entering the dimly lit room, rousing music welcomed visitors to the dance floor. The lively organ music of Danny White, one of the more popular entertainers, featured his renditions of the popular hits of the day. With the lights always low and the sounds always sweet, the Creole Room was perfect for dancing the night away.

The Julep Room

The Julep Room was a lounge located in the bottom level of the Bayou Inn, which is now Aunt Jenny's Catfish Parlour in Ocean Springs. A jukebox in the corner provided the music for dancing or just sharing a drink at one of the booths. The atmosphere was enhanced by the glow of red lights in the low ceiling, giving everything an almost dreamlike

The Creole Room. *Paul Jermyn collection.*

The Biloxi Hotel. *Paul Jermyn collection.*

quality. Patrons could walk with their dates from the lounge outside down to the hotel pavilion overlooking the bayou. Music from the club played over outside speakers near the water. Romantic songs like "Al Di La" by singer Emilio Pericoli from the movie *Rome Adventure* made the date an unforgettable experience. One could almost imagine Troy Donahue and Suzanne Pleshette standing alongside, locked in an embrace. Rumor was that Elvis often stopped by the Julep Room when he was staying at the Gulf Hills Dude Ranch not far away.

The Beach Water Club

The Beach Water Restaurant and Club was one of the best places to hear some of our great local bands. Often the groups that played there were larger than at most other venues. At times, there would be as many as ten to twelve musicians in the band, along with several horns. It was located on the south side of Highway 90 between the Bungalow and Holley's Triple X service station. The Beach Water was eventually the site of the *Biloxi Belle* casino boat, one of the first casino boats on the coast.

The Peppermint Lounge

The Peppermint Lounge was a rockin' place to dance. Located on Pat H. Harrison Avenue, later called Veterans Avenue, the Peppermint Lounge was named after the popular New York nightclub. Like the club in New York, Biloxi's club had a somewhat questionable group of patrons, including hookers, transvestites and other interesting characters.

Charlie's Hideaway

Just across the railroad tracks north of the Peppermint Lounge was a club called Charlie's Hideaway. On the south side of the building, separated from the regular Charlie's Hideaway, was a club called the Boom Boom Room. Charlie's was a dinner and dance club for the older crowd, while the Boom Boom Room was a rollicking bar for young adults. Appearing nightly at the club was a black female singer called Lollipop. She became famous for playing piano and singing risqué songs. She was quite bawdy for the '50s. Her piano was located in the center of a wraparound bar. The lights were low, and Lollipop would sing her signature version of the happy birthday song to any of the patrons who were celebrating their special day. She would sing "Happy Birthday," inserting the birthday person's name in the standard song along with suggestive innuendoes characteristic of her other songs.

Café KoKo

Café KoKo was located in a small motel on the south side of Highway 90 on West Beach Biloxi near Camellia Street. The club was next door to the Sun-n-Sand, one of the coast's most popular motels and entertainment centers. The café, owned by Harry and Ruth Meier, had an eclectic menu that included Chinese, Mexican and American cuisine. Café KoKo was best known for its famous organ bar featuring the world-renowned organist and singer Princess Whitecloud.

Princess Neioma Whitecloud was the daughter of a council chief of the Oglala Sioux Indians. She had received the title of "Princess" when she was a young woman in recognition for her work in bringing much-needed water to the Rosebud Reservation in South Dakota.

Princess Whitecloud.

There were several popular organists in the clubs along the Gulf Coast in the '50s, such as Alex Ortega at Trader John's and Oakley West at the Buena Vista, but none had the musical background of Princess Whitecloud. Few on the coast realized how accomplished she was. Princess Whitecloud studied music at the Darmstadt and Frankfurt Konservatoriums of Musik in Germany, Juilliard in New York, Sherwood in Chicago and Rutgers University in New Jersey. She was the featured organist for a while with the Glenn Miller Band and was signed exclusively with MCA, performing at such prestigious venues as the Hollywood Bowl.

Princess Whitecloud was one of the coast's true treasures and performed exclusively at Café Koko for almost ten years. During her shows, she encouraged sing-alongs and would play requests into the wee hours of the morning five nights a week. She knew all of the college fight songs and would gladly play any one of them when asked. During each of her performances, she kept her little Chihuahua, Fifi, seated by her side. During the day, she taught organ, piano and voice at Werlein's for Music in Biloxi.

She was proud of her Indian heritage and was known for riding in the Biloxi Mardi Gras parades in full-feathered headdress, followed behind by the Biloxi High School Indians marching band in full Indian outfits.

Elsie's Bar

Elsie's was a small bar just south of the railroad tracks on the west side of Cowan Road. On the inside of Elsie's was a long bar along the left wall, while on the right were three pinball machines. Music was always playing on the jukebox nearby. The rest of the bar was filled with small tables for couples and singles hoping to meet up with that right person.

Elsie's happy hour was between 6:00 and 9:00 p.m. and featured twenty-five-cent mixed drinks. The cheap drinks ensured the place would be packed. Elsie, her husband, Lanny, and their son-in-law, Bob, kept the mixed drinks

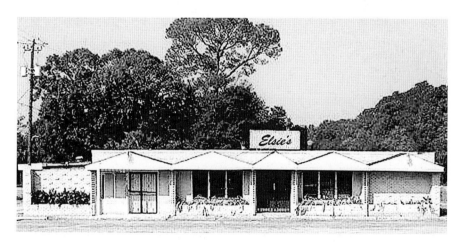

Elsie's bar.

coming at a speed that was incredible. The regulars had only to hold up their fingers to let Bob know how many more drinks were needed, and within seconds, he would have them at the table.

Spider's Bar

Spider's Bar was located on East Beach Boulevard at Dolan Avenue. Parking for Spider's was at the Standard Oil station across the street. The entrance to Spider's was on the left side of the building. The interior décor was typical of a beach bar, with neon beer signs adding a colorful glow to the walls. Above the bar, a Schlitz sign flickered as if the neon bulb was about to blow. The bar was U-shaped, although most of the guys crowded around the left side near the restrooms so they could check out the girls going by. On the east side of the bar, two pinball machines were always in play.

Like Elsie's bar, Spider's served twenty-five-cent mixed drinks during happy hour. Happy hour at Spider's started at five o'clock, a full hour before any other bar on the coast. Spider's also had good food. Many people came just for its house special, the Wheelburger, a hamburger to die for. There were also other great items on the menu that ensured a good lunch business.

On New Year's Day 1963, the original Spider's was destroyed by fire. It reopened on the lot where the Standard Oil station once stood. Spider's continued on as a popular watering hole for several years after it was rebuilt.

The Fiesta

The sign read, "Fiesta at the Fiesta," and that is what it was. It was one of the best places on the Gulf Coast to listen to live music, dance, place a few bets and just have a good time. At the time, it was the largest dance club on the coast, featuring four bars and four dance floors. There was an all-girl revue and go-go girls dancing in cages. The music featured folk singers like the Brandywine Singers, rock bands like Vince Vance and the Valiants, lounge bands like Jerry Mayburn and Latin bands like Betty Lopez and the Latin Stars. One of its featured drinks was a hurricane, served in a similar glass as the famous one at Pat O'Brien's bar in New Orleans. A Caribbean-style

The Fiesta lounge.

straw hat was given to each person after paying the modest cover charge. Fiesta hats were seen all over the coast. Live entertainment! Great fun! Fiesta at the Fiesta!

The Flame Drive-In

The Flame Drive-In was located southeast of Gulfport High School within a half-block walking distance. Some students looking for an alternative to school cafeteria food would walk to the Flame for lunch. The Flame Drive-In was quick, and the po'boy sandwiches were delicious. The Flame was also a great oyster bar. Men would stop by on their way home for fresh oysters straight off the boats.

Trader John's

Trader John's, located at the Cabana Beach Hotel, was a favorite college hangout. It featured great folk singers, with a hootenanny every Monday night. Folk music was riding a wave of popularity at that time. One of the memorable characteristics of the club was the basket of oranges, lemons and limes that hung over the bar. These fresh fruits were used in all of the drinks. One of the most popular drinks was a screwdriver made with fresh-squeezed oranges from the basket.

The Hambone Club/The Orbit Club

The Hambone Club located on the Pass Road in Handsboro was a popular nightclub in the late '40s and early '50s before it changed to the equally popular Orbit Club. The Orbit Club was remembered for the neon rocket sign that was positioned over the front. The building had a couple of wooden steps up from the parking lot to the entrance. Patrons parked their cars under the large oaks in the oyster-shelled front yard. There was always some lively music playing, and on occasion, big names like Jim Owen would drop by to jam with the regular band.

The Vapors

The Vapors was a large nightclub on the beach east of the Broadwater Beach Hotel. It was one of the most popular and active dance clubs on the coast for teens and young adults. Extremely loud, smoky and crowded, it featured live bands like Vince Vance and the Valiants. Before photo IDs, creating an acceptable ID card was easy, leading to many suspiciously young-looking patrons. The Vapors was destroyed by Hurricane Camille in 1969 and rebuilt before finally being destroyed by a fire on May 20, 1971.

LIVE ENTERTAINMENT

Gus Stevens Seafood Restaurant and Buccaneer Lounge

Gus Stevens was the premier supper club in the South and the ultimate place to take a date for any special occasion. The finest western prime meats were imported from Chicago to serve in full-course dinners starting at $1.50. A double sirloin steak for two was only $6.00. For only $1.25, you could get the original barbecued shrimp on a stick.

Gus Stevens had the finest dance orchestra anywhere and was the only club on the coast that brought in such headline entertainment as Mel Tormé, Judy Garland, Mamie Van Doran, Brother Dave Gardner, Andy Griffith, Johnny Rivers, Jerry Lee Lewis, Jerry Clower, Jerry Van Dyke and, of course, Jayne Mansfield. There were three floor shows nightly at 9:30 p.m., 11:00 p.m. and 2:00 a.m. Gus Stevens also provided slot machines and other forms of gambling for the patrons. There was never a cover charge, and the coffee shop and dining room were open twenty-four hours a day.

Sie's Place

For country music fans, Sie's Place, owned by Sie Simon, was the place to be. Sie's slogan was "Where Nice People Come to Have a Nice Time." Located on the corner of Division and Reynoir Streets in Biloxi, Sie's Place became known as the number-one country western club throughout the '40s, '50s and '60s. We all went there to dance. There was the Biloxi Shuffle, or the Sie Simon Shuffle, as we called it. And there was also the popular "broom" dance, where brooms were substituted for our dancing partners. It was not uncommon to see stars there like Marty Robbins, Jerry Lee Lewis, Minnie Pearl, the Everly Brothers and even a young Elvis. Many of the big names that were playing at Gus Stevens club would drop over to Sie's after their sets. Along with the music, patrons enjoyed slot machines and blackjack, since illegal gambling flourished in many of the clubs and hotels on the beach at that time. Sie's closed in 1973.

Gus Stevens supper club.

Places to Go and Things to See

The Beach

The fourteen miles of beautiful sand beach is the number-one attraction along the Mississippi Gulf Coast. With the arrival of warm weather in the spring, we all headed to the beach with blankets and transistor radios blasting out the top tunes on WTIX or WNOE. The parking bays along Highway 90 made it convenient to stop anywhere from Pass Christian to Biloxi. During the day, the white sand beach was dotted with colorful towels, while at night, large bonfires pointed the way to beach parties or private get-togethers—just far enough away from the road to be very private. Drinking beer, dancing in the sand and playing beach volleyball were perfect ways to spend time together.

Mississippi Deep Sea Fishing Rodeo

The Mississippi Deep Sea Fishing Rodeo is a salt- and fresh-water fishing competition held annually during the first week of July as part of the Fourth of July celebration on the Mississippi Gulf Coast.

In the beginning, it was conceived to be a local fishing competition open to all ages to promote fishing on the Gulf Coast. The event was an instant success, becoming the highlight of the Fourth of July celebration from the start. In 1953, Mississippi governor Hugh L. White proclaimed the rodeo to be the state's official fishing tournament. This decree made the results of the competition the state's official fishing records. In 1958, under the leadership of Robert L. Rice, the rodeo developed from a local event into one of the largest sportfishing annual attractions in the world.

The weeklong celebration is far different today than it was in the '50s, before the modern Rice Pavilion. Many of us remember the sawdust floors under a circus tent, the fishy smells in the salty air and the day's catch on display on beds of crushed ice. To those of us who were not fishermen, the carny games of chance and the thrilling carnival rides were the greatest draws, with the gigantic fireworks display capping the final evening's events.

Today, the Mississippi Deep Sea Fishing Rodeo is still free to all entrants, with the number of those participating exceeding three thousand each

Harrison County's twenty-six-mile-long sand beach. Shown here is Miss Pat Koenenn, Gulfport Chamber of Commerce, 1952. *Clayton Rand Papers, Manuscripts Division, Special Collections Department, Mississippi State University Libraries.*

Mississippi governor Hugh L. White proclaimed the rodeo to be the state's official fishing tournament. *Paul Jermyn collection.*

year. Prizes are awarded in twenty-eight different categories. A first and second prize is awarded on the final day, including a king and queen fisherman trophy.

Triangle Lanes

The Triangle Lanes on 25th Avenue was the first modern bowling facility on the coast. Bowling had become popular on television, creating a large demand for the sport. There were bowling leagues and tournaments that catered to church groups and other civic-minded organizations. Many stay-at-home wives enjoyed leagues during the morning that took the place of their regular bridge parties.

Mrs. Rippy's Skating Rink

Almost everyone who lived in the '50s has fond memories of Mrs. Eva Rippy's skating rink on the corner of 17th Street and 26th Avenue. Every Saturday, we would go zooming around the floor, hand in hand, moving with the rhythm of the organ music—music we would have never listened to on our radios but was the perfect accompaniment for the skaters. "Mom" Rippy's grandson, Bill, managed the pacing of the music from slow to party time, playing music from Eva's stack of 78 rpm records. The rink was festively decorated with colorful balloons floating up to the ceiling. Special events kept the atmosphere hopping while we did the hokey pokey or the limbo.

Biloxi-Gulfport Amusement Park

The Biloxi-Gulfport Amusement Park, located on the south side of Highway 90 at Pat Harrison Avenue, was fun. We loved the carnival atmosphere, the small-scale mom-and-pop rides, the games of chance and the calliope music blaring from large speakers attached to telephone poles high above the midway. A small Ferris wheel ran continuously, taking us high above the beach. The colorful characters who ran the games would let us win just enough to keep us coming back. The park opened in 1955 but was destroyed by Hurricane Camille in 1969. It was reopened under new owners and ran until the early '80s, when it closed for good.

Poston's Carpet Golf

Poston's was the first miniature golf course on the coast. It was so popular with both adults and children that we usually found ourselves waiting in line for a turn to play. At that time, there were no interesting sculptures like the dinosaur or the Buddha that would later become icons of Goofy Golf.

Goofy Golf

In 1958, after Poston's Carpet Golf closed, Lee Koplin opened Goofy Golf in the Poston's location on the beach. Before Goofy Golf, miniature golf was fun but not exciting. That all changed with the addition of windmills, water traps, tunnels, jumps and other obstacles that made miniature golf much more challenging. Koplin had developed a construction method that allowed him to create the dinosaur, the Buddha and other iconic Goofy Golf sculptures. Miniature golf was never better and was a great place to take a date.

Iconic Buddha sculpture at the Goofy Golf.

Eight Flags Deer Ranch

Eight Flags Deer Ranch was one of the most unique attractions on the coast. Started in 1962, it offered several tourist events. There was a petting zoo that allowed the visitors to feed and pet the tame deer that had been brought in from all over the country. Other attractions included a bird act featuring trained parrots and other exotic birds. The most exciting part of the Deer Ranch was the Red Dog Saloon, which was a replica of an old western saloon complete with a stage show and dancing girls. The saloon was part of a bigger set known as Six Gun Junction where cowboys staged realistic gunfights, shooting one another down in the streets as well as dramatically off the old buildings.

Marine Life Marinearium. *Paul Jermyn collection.*

Marine Life

The Marine Life Marinearium opened in Jones Park in 1956 with interactive exhibits that featured many forms of marine animals, including some species that were endangered. Marine Life was dedicated to the conservation and protection of the animals' environment, as well as educating the public. The experienced staff shared interesting information during the thrilling porpoise shows and other demonstrations that centered on some of the other animals.

Pontchartrain Beach

At the Beach, at the Beach, at Pontchartrain Beach, we'll have fun, we'll have fun every day of the week.

Everyone who lived in Gulfport and along the coast can still remember that catchy jingle. Pontchartrain Beach was the Six Flags of its day with amusement rides, concession stands and an entertaining stage show.

The clown's head at Pontchartrain Beach Amusement Park.

Pontchartrain Beach, located on the south shore of Lake Pontchartrain, had been around since the late '20s. Its founder, Harry Batt Sr., searched the world over for the newest, fastest and most exciting rides to add to the park. The biggest draw was the large wooden roller coaster called the Zephyr. Other rides included the Wild Maus, the haunted house, bumper cars, a Ferris wheel and more. There was also an authentic carousel that dated back to the late 1800s.

Live shows and concerts featured some of the nation's hottest stars, including an appearance by Elvis Presley. There was no additional charge for the shows, which were free to the visitors at Pontchartrain Beach.

Gulfport versus Biloxi Football

Gulfport was always a contender in high school football for the top spot against our rivals—Meridian, Pascagoula, Brookhaven, McComb, Natchez, Picayune, Moss Point, Hattiesburg, Laurel and Columbia—and our archenemy, Biloxi. There was also varsity basketball and tennis coached by Victor Allgood, track by Tommy Caldwell, golf by Ben Jones and baseball and football coached by Lindy Callahan.

The football competition between Gulfport and Biloxi was fierce and always resulted in some form of drama. But nothing could compare to the forty-third annual Thanksgiving Day classic that was held in 1958. The game was looking good for Gulfport. The crowd went wild when the Gulfport Commodores intercepted a pass by the Biloxi Indians. A fumble by the Indians on the next play allowed the Commodores to take the lead at the end of the first half. There was tension in the air and everyone could feel it, even in the stands.

At the start of the second half, the Indians brought in a whole new team. These new players were out for blood as they waged a furious battle against Gulfport. The second half was all about Biloxi, and even though the Commodores fought a valiant fight to the end, the Indians beat the Commodores by a score of 19–10.

Needless to say, tempers were flaring, and after the game ended, fights among the players began to break out on the field. There were some minor injuries, resulting in suspensions and visits to the principal's office the next morning.

Because of this horrible display of sportsmanship, the school officials decided it was best to suspend any further games between Gulfport and Biloxi. In 1968, the restriction was finally lifted, and the two teams were able to face each other once again. And while this game marked an end to a long and bitter feud between the two cities, it was a bittersweet moment for Gulfport, which lost that game also. Biloxi beat Gulfport 26–14, and the duel has continued.

Chapter 10

GAMBLING ON THE MISSISSIPPI GULF COAST

*G*ambling became legal in certain parts of Mississippi in the 1990s. For the people who grew up in Gulfport in the '50s, however, widespread gambling was nothing new. Gambling had been a thriving business on the Gulf Coast since the 1930s along a strip of glittering neon lights and exotic dance clubs.

The coast was never typical of the rest of the state. Cotton fields and stately plantations like those in *Gone with the Wind* are not part of our lives on the Gulf. Some would even say we were more accepting of ways that were condemned throughout most of the Bible Belt. But while there was a degree of tolerance for illegal gambling and booze, scandals and crooked payoffs to law enforcement officials were an integral part of the otherwise laissez-faire situation.

Gambling on the Gulf Coast goes back to the era of the Great Depression. Like the rest of the country, businesses here were struggling to keep their doors open. Everyone was looking for ways to pump up the economy and to protect what little they had. Pete Martin Sr. was one of those who recognized a golden opportunity. Martin had made a fortune as a successful gambler, and he knew how profitable gambling could be. Using proceeds from his winnings, he invested on the Gulf Coast, building the iconic Broadwater Beach Hotel with gambling money specifically as an outlet for his gaming activities.

The Broadwater was a four-story building in the Art Deco style popular on Miami's South Beach. In addition, Martin built a six-hundred-foot fishing

The Biloxi strip, 1950s.

The Broadwater Beach Hotel. *Paul Jermyn collection.*

The Broadwater Beach Hotel pavilion. *Paul Jermyn collection.*

pier with a small bathhouse across the highway on the beach with the same Art Deco look as the hotel. This pavilion contained a barbershop, a snack bar, a beauty shop and Martin's first gambling equipment.

With the success of the Broadwater Beach, gambling began to spread all along the Mississippi Gulf Coast. The major hotels and even smaller businesses such as grocery stores and service stations offered slot machines.

Harry Bennett, like Pete Martin, was also a professional gambler. He moved to the coast in 1943. Bennett bought the Bob Thompson Lounge and changed the name to the Paddock Club. The club became a driving force in illegal gambling on the Mississippi Gulf Coast. Located at the intersection of Camellia Street and Highway 90, the Paddock Club was close to other popular clubs like the Stable, the Fiesta, the Plaza Club and Gus Stevens. Although gambling and booze were illegal in the state, the clubs on the coast openly offered both. Along with the bar and featured entertainment in the front, the Paddock Club had craps, roulette, dice tables and slots in the back.

Illegal gambling flourished on the coast throughout the '40s, and as a result, the community began to wage attacks against the clubs and their owners. A group of local ministers called the Biloxi Protestant Ministerial Association banded together with some citizens to complain that the laws against gambling were not being enforced. As a result of the large amount of publicity generated by the group, law enforcement

The Paddock Club. *Paul Jermyn collection.*

officials were forced to at least appear to act. These same officials had been taking bribes from the clubs and, therefore, had little stomach for any meaningful shutdown.

In 1951, the U.S. Senate formed a committee to investigate organized crime in the United States, including illegal gaming on the coast. Headed by Senator Estes Kefauver from Tennessee, the Kefauver Committee traveled all over the country.

As it turned out, Keesler Air Force Base had the greatest impact on the group's effort. This was somewhat of a dichotomy since it was the Keesler airmen who were the greatest supporters of the clubs. When some of these young servicemen complained to their parents that they were losing their money in the crooked clubs, the parents began to question what was going on in Biloxi. Many sent letters to Senator Kefauver directing the committee's attention to the Gulf Coast.

Kefauver's visit confirmed what the parents had reported but did not lead to any meaningful result. The committee took no action but recommended that the City of Biloxi no longer tolerate the illegal activity. For a short time after the committee left the coast, there was a weak attempt to shut down the gambling. Laz Quave, the mayor of Biloxi, promised to enforce the laws, and during his time in office, there were several arrests. Although this did have a slight effect, it did not eliminate illegal gambling from the coast.

In August 1952, Keesler Air Force Base placed the clubs off-limits to the airmen. In April 1953, Mississippi governor Hugh White threatened to close all of the clubs if the Harrison County sheriff did not act. Bennett bowed to the warning and closed the Paddock Club but showed his defiance by opening the 5 O'Clock Club only months later. After Senator Estes Kefauver's committee attempted to shut down illegal gambling on the coast, Pete Martin moved his gambling operation across the highway from the Broadwater pavilion into the Broadwater Beach Hotel's main lobby.

On September 7, 1955, seven clubs and restaurants were raided and closed by order of Governor White. Bennett's 5 O'Clock Club was one of the first to be targeted. The others included the Broadwater Beach Hotel, Ray's Drive-In, Paradise Point, Shangri La, Fairchild's and the Pines. All were discovered to have illegal gambling equipment on their premises except for the Broadwater Beach Hotel, which had quit the gaming industry a year earlier.

In a show of action, longtime coast lawman Bravo E. Woodcock dumped nine slot machines on the corner of 2nd and Clark Streets in Pass Christian. The machines had been confiscated a week earlier. Using a double-sided axe, Woodcock hacked away at the machines. Coins from the pay-off tubes flew everywhere as local children scrambled for the nickels. The incident drew a record crowd.

With the closure of his 5 O'Clock Club, Harry Bennett left the coast for New Orleans. In the late 1950s, he returned to the coast with a partner, Dewey D'Angelo, to open the Red Carpet Club. The Red Carpet became known as a "Juice Joint," which in gambling parlance meant the club was crooked. The "juice" was a large electromagnet that was built into the floor under the craps table. When the operator flipped a switch that was kept in his pocket, the dice could be controlled. The Red Carpet Club operated for at least seven years before being forced to close in 1965.

East of the Red Carpet Club was the Ace of Clubs, owned by Jewel Garriga. The rumor is that an elderly couple built the club for Jewel's husband, Asa Garriga Jr. The old man loved Asa as if he were a son. That all changed, however, when the man discovered Asa had been acting against him. So in retaliation, the irate man signed the club over to Asa's wife, Jewel, who immediately divorced Asa. The club's name was then changed to the Show Club.

Like the Red Carpet Club, the Ace of Clubs was also known for its crooked gambling tables. A scam called the "hat" was often pulled on unsuspecting patrons. The staff would target a customer sitting alone at the bar. One of the B Girls would start casually talking with him to see where he was from. The club would only pull the "hat" scam on someone from out of town to lessen the chance of any reprisal. Once the scam was given the green light, an employee of the bar, posing as another customer, would come into the club and sit on a stool next to the target. As they talked, the employee (customer) would suggest that the bartender roll some dice for the price of his drinks. The bartender would of course refuse, but after more prodding, the bartender would offer an alternative: he would consider playing a hand of five-card stud for the drinks. To make the scam seem more legit, the bartender would ask the target, as an innocent observer, to shuffle the deck. Before the bartender dealt the

A possible target of the hat scam. *Paul Jermyn collection.*

cards, however, he would suggest that the target also take a hand just to make the bet more interesting. The bartender, who had palmed some winning cards, dealt a few to the target, making his hand look like it was going to be a sure thing. The other customer (employee), who knew the target's hand appeared to be a winner, would suggest that the target pressure the bartender to also put up some cash in addition to the free drinks. His chances looked so good that the target almost always fell for the scam. The bartender would act reluctant to put up any money at first to avoid any suspicion but would finally agree. Of course, the poor customer would lose and generally just thought it was due to his bad luck. The other customer (employee) would then take his drinks, leave the club and wait for the next sucker.

Most all of the clubs used shills to work the people. These were beautiful women who would engage the men in conversation at the gaming tables. They would try to cajole the men into placing bets for the women with the customer's money. The object was to get the men to lose their money and possibly leave a large tip for the shill.

Although the Friendship House Restaurant has a long-standing reputation as a favorite family eating place, it was also known for its slot machines during the '50s. Other clubs and restaurants that featured gaming activities were the Raven Club, the Fiesta Club, Trader John's, Sea N' Sirloin Restaurant and the Cabana Beach Motel.

Several of the clubs featured Las Vegas–style shows with bands, dancing girls and strippers. Probably the most noteworthy show was the Jewel Box Review at the Gay Paree. The Jewel Box Review was a touring company that featured female impersonators. The revue, which had begun in 1939, was tremendously popular throughout the whole United States, running well into the 1960s. The troupe consisted of as many as twenty-five men transformed into gorgeous women. There was only one real woman in the show. She was the emcee, Miss Storme DeLaviere, who was also the only male impersonator in the review. Some of the stars of the show were Lyle Mack ("America's Most Beautiful Girl"), Pepper Cortez ("Boy with the Million Dollar Legs"), Jackie Starr ("America's Most Beautiful Man"), Gita Gilmore ("Male Mae West"), Selina Powers, Francis Stillman, Billie Hayes and Frank Bennett, among others.

Other clubs from that period that offered gambling were Chez Joey's, owned by Mike Gillich, later associated with the Dixie Mafia and the Sherry murder case in Biloxi; Bennie French's at Henderson Point on U.S. Highway 90 near the Bay St. Louis bridge; the Shangri-La; the

Selina Powers of the Jewel Box Review.

Key Club; and the Eight Day Lounge on Pat Harrison Avenue. In north Gulfport, up on Old Highway 49, there were the Beverly Lounge and the Hi-Hat Club.

The Golden Nugget, also owned by Mike Gillich, was next to the Gay Paree. The Golden Nugget Club started out as the very popular Golden Nugget Bingo Hall. In the early '60s, the bingo hall was split into two clubs. Gillich kept the larger portion on the west side of the building, which he called the Golden Nugget. Frank Schenck Sr. took the portion connected on the east side. Frank's club was very small. There was only a bar and a few stools, although it did have a long stage area behind the bar where the girls would perform. Frank Schenck Jr. opened the Taurus Steak House adjacent to the small club.

In 1962, the state adjutant general, William Wilson, attempted again to shut down illegal gambling on the coast. Wilson directed an attack on three of the popular nightclubs in Biloxi. Three six-man teams of National Guardsmen raided the Key Club, the Gay Paree and the Spot, destroying dice tables, roulette wheels, blackjack and poker games, slot machines and liquor valued at $25,000.

James Porter, owner of the Spot, and Dewey D'Angelo were fined $138. In addition, Porter lost gambling equipment valued at $7,500 and illegal alcohol valued at $3,000.

The Harrison County sheriff, Curtis O. Dedeaux, who was known to benefit from the black-market payoffs, tried to downplay the action, claiming that Governor Barnett authorized the raid for publicity.

In 1963, the raids continued, this time led by IRS agents. The *Daily Herald* reported that on April 4, fifteen pinball machines valued at $10,000 were confiscated. John E. Montgomery, the special agent in charge, reported that these were part of a total of forty-eight pinball machines that had recently been seized because the owners had failed to pay an annual federal tax of $250 on each machine. Three of the pinball machines were taken from the Pink Poodle, six were from Sooky's Lounge, one was from Kandy News and five came from the Archery Arcade. The other thirty-three pinball machines came from Cecil's Restaurant, Airmen News, Mickey's Billiard Center, the Greyhound Bus Station, Geno's Café, Star News and Tobacco, Joe's Elbow Room and Roy's News and Tobacco Store. On November 2, 1953, the IRS estimated there were between five hundred and one thousand pinball machines scattered throughout Harrison County.

Things were beginning to unravel in the mid-'60s when Asa Garriga Jr. was arrested and convicted of violating the White Slavery Traffic Law and sentenced to the federal penitentiary. According to the *Daily Herald* of October 27, 1965, Garriga was one of seven witnesses for the prosecution in federal court against former Harrison County sheriff Curtis Dedeaux. Dedeaux was charged with accepting graft from bar operators, income tax evasion and giving false information to the Internal Revenue Service for the years 1960–62. In his testimony, Garriga accused Sheriff Dedeaux of having taken protection money from him in order for Garriga to continue his illegal activities in slot machines, prostitution and alcohol.

As late as 1968, the charade continued. Clubs still offered backroom gambling, and the officials continued to conduct their phony raids. This was evident when Harrison County sheriff Luther Patton staged a high-profile raid in 1968, destroying all the slot machines that were seized. This was only an attempt to appease the citizens who were fed up with illegal gambling. Patton proved to be a part of the shady system when he was later convicted of tax evasion and had to pay $120,000 in taxes and penalties on unreported income for the years 1968–72. That money represented kickbacks and bribes that he had received from gambling interests.

Ultimately, it was the force of nature that put an end to illegal gambling on the Gulf Coast. On August 19, 1969, Hurricane Camille hit the strip, destroying everything in its path, including the gambling clubs and bars. Gaming along the coast never recovered until gambling in the state was finally legalized in the 1990s.

Those of us who lived in Gulfport during the '50s and '60s remember the exciting nightlife, the bands, the dancing, the unchecked IDs. We experienced an exciting time in Gulf Coast history. As teenagers coming of age, we cruised the strip in our cool cars from Bay St. Louis to Biloxi with our hot dates by our sides. We hit the clubs and the bars, and we grew up way before our time.

Chapter II

MOMENTS TO REMEMBER

One word or phrase can trigger a memory every bit as vivid as any old photograph. The following words are the essence of growing up in Gulfport in the '50s. Many of these impressions could never have been captured on film, but hopefully they will remind some readers of a special moment in their lives.

SNAPSHOTS OF GULFPORT

The smell of fresh bread wafting from the Colonial Bakery on Pass Road
Doing the limbo at Mrs. Rippy's Skating Rink
Midnight bowling at the Triangle Lanes
Pigeons strutting about at the bus stop in front of McCrory's
Cy Rape Drug Store on 25th Avenue
Eight flags monument between Gulfport and Biloxi
The Purple Lantern—the most exotic place on earth
Watching the broom dance at Sie's Place
The Gypsy saying, "If you drink, don't drive, and if you drive, don't drink"
Gigging flounders at night in the shallow waters of the Gulf
The aroma of coffee in the old A&P store on 13th Street
Rooftop dancing at the Buena Vista Hotel
Paying the twenty-five-cent toll to cross the Bay St. Louis bridge

The Colonial Baking Company. *Paul Jermyn collection.*

The Purple Lantern. *From Nels Anderson.*

Gigging flounders in the Gulf. *Paul Jermyn collection.*

The Buena Vista Hotel. *Paul Jermyn collection.*

Christmas packages from Shamis wrapped in black paper with huge gold bows and sprinkled with fake snow

Riding the escalator at Sears

Bonfires on the beach

Buying brightly colored chicks for Easter from Wayne Feed Store

Watching the mechanical figures in the window of Fasold's Jewelry Store

Christmas lights strung across the streets of downtown Gulfport

Learning to water ski at Gulfport Lake and attempting to slalom

Eating those scrumptious soft rolls for lunch at the school cafeteria

Eating chips of ice at the Gulfport Ice Company

Watching Saturday morning serials at the Gulf Theatre

Remembering flat tops, sock hops and penny loafer shoes

Crabbing from one of the piers on the beach

Fender skirts, whitewall tires and wire curb feelers

Ovaltine chocolate drink and Captain Midnight decoder rings

The pungent smell of mimeograph ink

Laughing at Mr. Winstead's lame jokes in his math class

Learning to play the Flutophone with the high school bandleader, Carl Balius

Movie-Tone News and cartoons at the Paramount Theatre before the main feature

Boiling water in the percolator to make coffee

Shooting snooker at Totsy's Pool Hall

"I will not talk in class" one hundred times on the blackboard

Playing the pinball machines at the Palm Drive-In on 22nd Avenue

Watching the men shuck oysters at the Flame Drive-In

Feeding the ducks at the Colonial Bakery pond

Painting landscapes in Mrs. Gridley's art classes at the GRC

Smelling the leather and polish at Cabibi's Shoe Repair

Cleaning the chalkboard erasers after school

Sunday afternoon drives with the family, ending with marshmallow sundaes at Stone's Ice Cream

Pulling the choke knob out on the car to start it in cold weather

Cruisin' through the Park & Eat

Ordering mixed drinks at the White Cap Drive-In

Wearing a straw hat from the Fiesta

Reciting a poem in front of Mrs. Evans's English class

Burning leaves in the backyard

Sears had the only escalator in Gulfport. Downtown Gulfport, 1965. *Clayton Rand Papers, Manuscripts Division, Special Collections Department, Mississippi State University Libraries.*

Christmas lights were strung across the streets for decoration. *Clayton Rand Papers, Manuscripts Division, Special Collections Department, Mississippi State University Libraries.*

Totsy D'Angelo. *From Judith D'Angelo.*

The GRC (Gulfport Recreation Center). *Clayton Rand Papers, Manuscripts Division, Special Collections Department, Mississippi State University Libraries.*

The Hotel Markham grand stairway. *Paul Jermyn collection.*

Using the horizontal hold knob to keep the television picture from rolling
  up or down
Defrosting the refrigerator once a week because ice would build up inside
Dancing at the Creole Room
Drying clothes on lines in the backyard
Trick-or-treating with our friends on Halloween—without our parents
Riding the cage elevator in the Hewes Building
Brass spittoons on the floor in the old Hancock Bank Building
Dances at the old Gulfport Yacht Club with Johnny Elmer and the Rockets
Cotillion ball at the Hotel Markham
"Rejoice dear hearts..." Brother Dave Gardner at Gus Stevens
Waiting for the Hummingbird at the L&N depot with our bags lined up
  along the tracks
Jivin' to Ray Fournier and His Rockin' Rebels singing "Cherry Pie"
Enjoying picnics at the old Cable Bridge

Chapter 12

A GENERATION GROWS UP

The generation in Gulfport during the golden era had a hunger for the future. In retrospect, our visions might have seemed overly innocent, but as we moved from the '50s into the '60s, we transformed everything. Unlike past generations, we found ourselves with leisure time. We had our own spending money. We drove our own cars. And we were a growing force of societal change.

The changes were so dramatic as to make the '50s look embarrassingly naïve and shallow. Baby boomers were coming of age, and we were rejecting just about everything associated with our parents' generation. With the introduction of the birth control pill, "free love" became an accepted norm. This changed everything as young girls no longer had to fear getting into trouble.

The free spirit that began with the Beatniks of the '50s expanded with the hippies. Musical groups like the Beatles and others were at the forefront of the social upheaval. We experimented with drugs and radical new ideas, while gurus like Dr. Timothy Leary prompted us to "turn on, tune in and drop out." Rock music was central to the movement, with the musicians becoming political activists as well as performers. Much of what we knew was no longer the same, but the environment gave us the conditions for arguably one of the greatest periods in America's history. Although we can't go back, I consider it a blessing to have been part of the golden age of Gulfport. It was an era in which we saw a sleepy coastal town become the second-largest city in Mississippi. Growing up in Gulfport was a fantastic journey, and we were all along for the ride.

BIBLIOGRAPHY

Ariès, Philippe. *Centuries of Childhood: A Social History of Family Life*. New York: Alfred A. Knopf, 1962.

Bailey, Beth L. *From Front Porch to Back Seat: Courtship in Twentieth-Century America*. Baltimore: Johns Hopkins University Press, 1993.

Belfrage, Sally. *Un-American Activities: A Memoir of the Fifties*. New York: HarperPerennial, 1995.

Bernard, Shane K. *Swamp Pop: Cajun and Creole Rhythm and Blues*. Jackson: University Press of Mississippi, 1996.

Black, Henry W. *Gulfport: Beginnings and Growth*. Bowling Green, KY: Riverdell Publications, 1986.

Christenson, Peter G., and Donald F. Roberts. *It's Not Only Rock & Roll: Popular Music in the Lives of Adolescents*. Cresskill, NJ: Hampton Press, Inc, 2004.

Clark, Dick, Fred Bronson and Ray Smith. *Dick Clark's* American Bandstand. New York: Collins Publishers, 1997.

Clark, Dick, Jim Mones and Vincent Alabiso. *The Fantastic 50's: When Fads, Fun and Flying Saucers Ruled the World*. New York: Times Books, 2009.

Connolly, Joseph. *All Shook Up: A Flash of the Fifties*. London: Cassell, 2000.

Derks, Scott. *This Is Who We Were: In the 1950s*. Amenia, NY: Grey House Publishing, 2013.

Dunar, Andrew J. *America in the Fifties*. Syracuse, NY: Syracuse University Press, 2006.

Ellis, Dan. *Gulfport: Celebration City*. Gulfport, MS: self-published, 2016.

————. *Gulfport Discovered*. Gulfport, MS: self-published, 1997.

Elrod, Bruce C. *Your Hit Parade*. Columbia, SC: Colonial Printing Co., 1982.

Epstein, Dan. *20ᵗʰ Century Pop Culture: The 50s*. Philadelphia: Chelsea House, 2000.

Erickson, Lynne Martin, and Kathryn Leide. *Remembering the Fifties*. Madison, WI: Bi-Folkal Productions, 2006.

Fatherley, Richard W., and David T. MacFarland. "The Birth of Top 40 Radio: The Storz Stations' Revolution of the 1950s and 1960s." 2014.

Fogg, Marnie. *1950s Fashion Print*. London: Batsford, 2010.

Gambling Vertical File. "Down South Magazine." May–June 1952 and September–October 1958; Mississippi Guide, December 8, 1937, Biloxi Public Library, Biloxi, Mississippi.

Green, Jonathon. *All Dressed Up: The Sixties and the Counterculture*. London: Pimlico, 1999.

Gulfport Area Chamber of Commerce. *Gulfport, Mississippi*. Lubbock, TX: Impact Map Co., 1977.

Gulfport Army Air Field. Baton Rouge, LA: Army and Navy Pub. Co., 1944.

Gulfport Field: Army Air Forces Training Command. Baton Rouge, LA: Army and Navy Pub. Co., 1943.

Gulfport, Mississippi: The Gateway to Panama. N.p.: Nabu Press, 2010.

Hancock Bank, Gulfport. *The Coast of Mississippi: Its Past and Progress*. Baton Rouge, LA: Moran Publishing Corporation, 1982.

Harrison County Observer (Gulfport, MS). "Facts About the Gulf Coast of Harrison County, Mississippi." 1985.

Hill, Laban Carrick. *America Dreaming: How Youth Changed America in the '60s*. New York: Little, Brown and Co., 2009.

Holt, Hazel. *History of Biloxi*. Biloxi, MS: First National Bank of Biloxi, 1968.

Hulme, Alison. *Consumerism on TV: Popular Media from the 1950s to the Present*. London: Routledge, 2016.

Keylin, Arleen. *The Fabulous Fifties*. New York: Arno Press, 1978.

LaFontaine, Bruce. *Classic Cars of the Fifties*. Mineola, NY: Dover Publications, Inc., 2004.

Lewis, W. Arthur. *Development Economics in the 1950s*. San Francisco: ICS Press, 1994.

Malko, George. *The One and Only Yo-yo Book*. New York: Avon, 1978.

Mance, Angelia L. "Gambling on the Gulf Coast: The Changing Cultural Landscape of Biloxi, Mississippi." Thesis, University of Alabama, 1996.

Massa, Dominic, and Angela Hill. *New Orleans TV: The Golden Age.* New Orleans, LA: Greater New Orleans Educational Television Foundation, 2003.

McGinnis, Tom. *A Girl's Guide to Dating and Going Steady.* New York: Doubleday, 1968.

Miller, Bettina. *Life in the Fabulous '50s: The Fads, Photos and Fun!* Greendale, WI: Reiman Media, 2009.

Nite, Norm N. *Rock On: The Illustrated Encyclopedia of Rock N' Roll: The Solid Gold Years.* New York: Harper & Row, 1982.

Oliver, Nola Nance. *The Gulf Coast of Mississippi.* New York: Hastings House, 1941.

Palladino, Grace. *Teenagers: An American History.* New York: BasicBooks, 1996.

Pearce, Christopher. *Fifties Source Book.* Kent, UK: Grange Books, 1998.

Radio Station WNOE. *The Wide and Wonderful's Top 50 Hit Paraders: WNOE 1060 on Your Dial: December 21, 1958.* New Orleans, LA: Radio Station WNOE, 1958.

R.L. Polk & Co. *Gulfport, Mississippi City Directory.* Richmond, VA: R.L. Polk & Co., 1900.

Sagolla, Lisa Jo. *Rock 'n' Roll Dances of the 1950s.* Santa Barbara, CA: Greenwood, 2011.

Salamone, Frank A. *Popular Culture in the Fifties.* Lanham, MD: University Press of America, 2001.

Sedgwick, Michael. *Cars of the Fifties and Sixties.* New York: Crescent Books, 1990.

Seventeen. "Cross Country Report on Teens." September 1959.

———. "How Much Do Boys Spend on Girls?" June 1959.

Shaw, Betty Hancock. *Gulfport.* Charleston, SC: Arcadia Publishing, 2011.

Smith, Wes. *The Pied Pipers of Rock 'n' Roll: Radio Deejays of the 50s and 60s.* Marietta, GA: Longstreet Press, 1989.

"United States. Illegal Gambling Activities Near Keesler Air Force Base. Hearings Before the Preparedness Subcommittee of the Committee on Armed Services, United States Senate, Eighty-Second Congress, First Session...October 22, 1951." Washington, D.C.: U.S. Government Printing Office, 1952.

WNOE: The James A. Noe Station, New Orleans. New Orleans, LA: Higgins Press, 1944.

ABOUT THE AUTHOR

*J*ohn Cuevas was born and raised in Gulfport, Mississippi, and has been researching Gulf Coast history since the 1950s. His family is one of the oldest pioneer families between Mobile and New Orleans. As creative director of his own advertising firm in Atlanta for over twenty-five years, he worked with some of the nation's top companies, wining gold awards in radio, television and print advertising. Cuevas has written numerous books and articles about the coast. His book *Cat Island* is considered to be the definitive history of this Gulf Coast barrier island. His book *Lost Gulfport* recalls the downtown business district the way it was in Gulfport's golden age, before much of it was destroyed by Hurricane Katrina in 2005. He was also nominated in 2019 for an award from the Mississippi Institute of Arts and Letters for his book *Discovering Cat Island*, a guide to the historic sites of the island.

Visit us at
www.historypress.com